BUILDING BLOCKS FOR SUNDAY SCHOOL GROWTH

Smyth & Helwys Publishing, Inc.
6316 Peake Road
Macon, Georgia 31210-3960
1-800-747-3016

Printed in the United States of America.

The paper used in this publication meets the
minimum requirements of American National
Standard for Information Sciences—Permanence
of Paper for Printed Library Materials.
ANSI Z39.48–1984. (alk. paper)

CIP Data on file with the Library of Congress

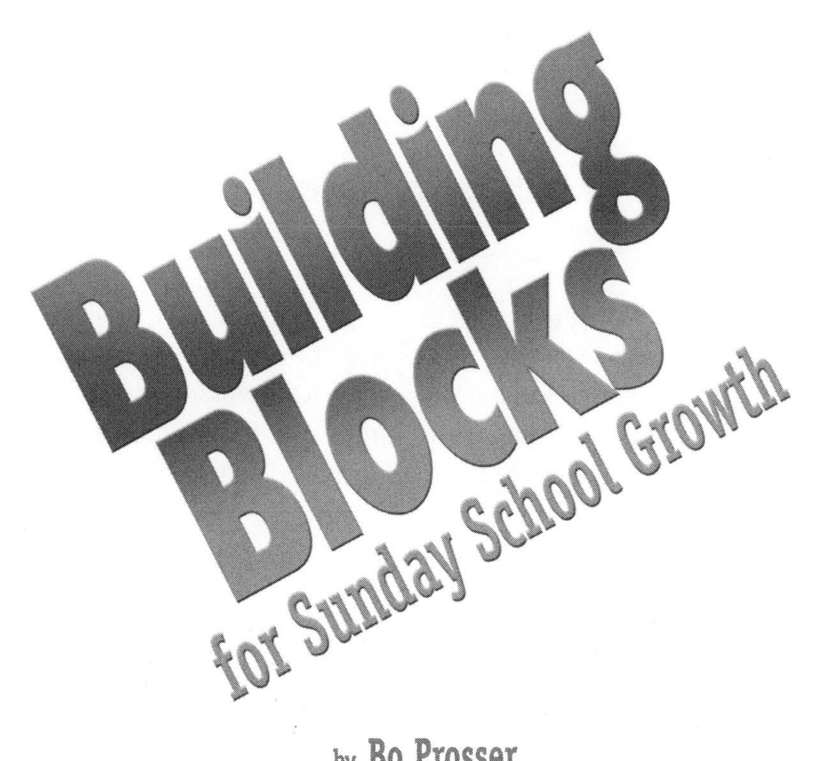

by **Bo Prosser**

with **Michael McCullar** and **Charles Qualls**

Dedications

From Bo Prosser:
With admiration to Michael and Charles for continued blessings and friendships. With love and admiration to the "Prosser Ladies" for continued affirmation. You are my wind! With appreciation to the Congregation of Providence Baptist Church, Charlotte for being a place of healing and grace.

From Michael McCullar:
To Lisa, Mallory and Jake...simply the reason!
To the Congregation of Johns Creeks Baptist Church...simply special!

From Charles Qualls:
For Elizabeth, partner and living model of grace.
To all the congregations I've journeyed with, thank for all you've taught me and all we're still to discover.

Table of Contents

Introduction

Trust God, Pray Daily, and Live On Bravely!

"Not another book on Sunday school!" exclaimed my friend when I told him we had this book in the works. "Who in the church cares about Sunday school in today's world?" he continued. "Sunday school is for old-timers. It's a thing of the past. I thought you were hip, with it, tuned in, an innovator!" he finished.

Whew! There is nothing like a bit of affirmation. However, I must admit that my friend got me thinking. Who does care about Sunday school? Is Sunday school just for "old-timers"? Can we be "hip, with it, and tuned in" and still believe in the ministry of the Sunday school?

My answer is an unequivocal, "Yes!"

The Bible teaching ministry in general and the Sunday school in particular are still vital parts of who we are in the church. Yes, innovation is needed. And that's where the idea for this book began: How can we honor tradition and introduce innovation into the Sunday school?

This is not just "another Sunday school" book. The ideas that we've suggested are not meant as a prescription for growth. Simply putting these ideas into an "overlay" of your current Sunday school will not automatically produce growth. Your task is to take these ideas and "baptize" them into your setting, applying what might work. We hope you will think about who you are and who you need to be. We hope you will be willing to try some of these approaches.

At the Center for Christian Education, we are committed to sharing a journey with you. My colleagues and I have tried to be practical and challenging. Our desire is that you and your church continue reaching out to those around you and reaching in to those with whom you now minister. Our desire is that you find relevant ideas and a balance for growth. As you grow in your vision, you grow in your motivation for serving others.

Many, like my friend above, are not too keen on the idea of church growth. Even fewer are still committed to the ministry of the Sunday school. We, the authors of this book, are still committed to both!

The local church is still relevant! Granted, our task today is more challenging than ever before; but God's people have never shied away from a challenge. While the challenge may be greater, the results may also be extraordinary. Numbers matter only in the way numbers represent people. And the numbers are staggering.

Most church watchers agree that somewhere around 66 percent of our nation is either non-believing or non-participating in matters of faith. Most church watchers agree that the church, as we know it, may cease to exist within the next fifty years. We cannot let that happen. God has called us to a wonderful mission. The church and the Sunday school are now and still can be relevant in the world in which we live. The form may need changing, but the function is needed now more than ever.

This book was being finalized during the days immediately following the tragedies of September 11, 2001. The nation was stunned by the evil of terrorism. Suddenly, a proud nation was humbled. In the aftermath, our churches were filled to overflowing for a couple of weeks. In times of tragedy, people desire a word from God. In times of evil, people seek a place of community. People are hungry as never before for a word from God and a community to which they can belong. The question is, what will we, as Christians, do? How will we respond?

Our contention is that the church and the Sunday school are the best-organized entities for helping others rediscover their faith in God. The church has a rich tradition for leading people into a meaningful relationship with the living Christ. The Sunday school has a rich tradition for helping others study and grow deeper in their faith and in their relationships with one another. But we cannot live only on tradition.

Our world is changing faster than most of us can comphrehend. Innovations have seen the advent of technology and instant communications in mind-boggling ways. The church has been slow to embrace technology. The church has been very slow to embrace innovation. But embrace innovation we must! We challenge you to embrace some of the ideas presented in this book and find ways to introduce innovative ideas into your church.

I am grateful to my two colleagues who have contributed to this writing. Much of the information in chapters 1 and 7 are from Michael McCullar. Michael is the Executive Pastor at Johns Creek Baptist Church in metro-Atlanta. Michael is an innovator and an educator. He challenges me almost every time we are together. He stretches me from my comfort zones. He was instrumental in the formation of the idea that would become The Center for Christian Education. I am grateful for his friendship and his challenges.

Charles Qualls provided much of the words in chapters 2 and 3. Charles is the Associate Pastor for Pastoral Care at Second Ponce de Leon in Atlanta. Charles keeps us grounded in our rich traditions while looking for growth ideas. His energy and insight have brought the idea of this book to fruition. Charles began his career as my intern, but, as often happens, the student has grown far beyond his teacher. I am grateful for his friendship and his grace.

I am grateful to other friends and mentors who continue to challenge my thoughts process. I am especially grateful to those who have reminded me that Sunday school is not important to everyone.

I am continually grateful for the support and partnership of my wife and our daughters. They continue to grant me grace when my travel schedule is over-committed and my mood may be cranky. These women have been and continue to be instrumental in who I am and who I am becoming. I am thankful to God for their love.

A cast of thousands has supported us in this effort! Dawn O'Neal and Jo-Ann Ingersoll helped me in the editing process. Their tireless efforts pointed out mistakes in grammar and in construction. The

Ministry Staff of Providence Baptist Church in Charlotte, NC, has shared ideas and given me much to think about. The Education Ministry team continued to challenge me to innovate when I would have preferred to stay within the safety of tradition. The congregation has also been a tremendous encouragement to me. This is a most loving and giving congregation of servants. They have given me freedom to innovate and grace when I missed the mark. They have encouraged me with the love of a strong tradition and challenged me with an equally strong spirit of innovation. I among all men am most richly blessed!

Thanks to Keith Gammons, our editor, and to the leadership team at Smyth & Helwys for their trust in me and affirmation of The Center for Christian Education.

To all of you—friends, family, colleagues—thank you for modeling "prepared for and cared for" during the development of our ideas.

Lastly, thanks be to God for his continuing grace and love. Until I find a better way, I will continue to be an advocate for the local church and for church growth. Until I find a better approach, the Sunday school will continue to be the ministry through which I try to make a difference. As we blend these six building blocks into a workable tool, perhaps we will find that what we most desire we've had in our midst all along! Until then, trust God, pray daily, and live on bravely!

— Bo Prosser
The Center for Christian Education
Providence Baptist Church
Charlotte, NC
October, 2001

Chapter One

The Once and Future Sunday School

When we were children, we couldn't wait to get to Sunday school. The smell of crayons and glue bring back fond memories. The feel of flannel boards and wooden blocks remind us of learning about Bible characters and sharing with friends. The sight of rough construction paper and tiny scissors reminds us of being accepted and loved by dedicated teachers. Seeing children carry those black, zippered Bibles with the cross dangling on the chain still evokes emotion from many of us. Hearing the slightly off-key sounds of "Jesus Loves Me" creates a moving "Kum-ba-ya" moment in our souls. Most of us in the church today hold a deep and abiding love for Sunday school. We belonged there, we made friends there, we felt loved there, and we were affirmed there. Sunday school was special!

Now we are adults, however, we seem to hold different feelings about Sunday school. Many adults still love the memory of childhood Sunday school; yet, we now deal with the reality that Sunday school often doesn't really meet our needs. We now encounter an institution that can no longer be seen as effective and vital to the overall church. The number of churches who consider Sunday school important to the work of their church program is declining. In a recent website chat room, several responders basically echoed the sentiment, "Who really cares about Sunday school today? That is for old-timers!"

True, the number of people attending this once (and still) vital ministry is also declining. True, worker dedication is at an all-time low. True, the maintenance of this ministry of learning and fellowship wears many ministers out. True, many of the "faithful few" remember the "glory days of Sunday school" and ask, "What's wrong?" But, do not be mistaken, the Sunday school is not dead!

Society today has relegated the church and especially the Sunday school to dinosaur status. A number of Sunday schools exist only for those already in the club, negating open acceptance and ministry to new people. Like it or not, the bottom line is simply this: The Sunday school as an institution is in trouble, and if not attended to soon, will likely diminish even more or fade away completely. But the Sunday school can still be a vital ministry contributing to the growth of your church.

What has caused this rampant decline in the once shining star of Christian Education ministry? While the answers are many and varied, we must go back to the late 1700s for a brief history of the Sunday school.

The Genesis of the Sunday School

The earliest form of a church-sponsored school has been traced to the efforts of Robert Raikes in England. Raikes saw far too many children in the streets of Gloucester, England, so he began a Sunday morning education experience. He enlisted some of the older women in his town to teach reading, writing, and praying to the poor and needy children of his town. Inspired by the work of Raikes, William Fox organized the Sunday School Union in 1785. His goal was to teach everyone in the world how to read and understand the Bible.

At the same time, in Virginia, William Elliot was beginning the modern Sunday school movement in America. In their original form, these schools were almost exclusively secular in teaching content. The teachers were paid for their services. Many church pastors served as the principals or headmasters and enlisted laypersons to oversee the schools.

Why was it called "Sunday School"? Simply because these church-sponsored programs met on Sunday. Sunday was the best day to reach the largest number of children. Due to the proliferation of working children, their only day off was Sunday. In those days, children were vital to the growing agricultural and industrial economies of their towns. This format for Sunday school worked well in its original intent. Since families were already at worship, a teaching experience was easily added to educate the children. The approach was also easily adapted to provide spiritual teaching.

The move to a more balanced mix of secular content and religious instruction came about in sweeping ways in 1825. At about the same time, the Sunday School Union was organized and literature specific to Christian teaching was developed. Both of these would help the Sunday school gain a national focus. In 1871, several denominations began working together to provide "uniform" lessons. By 1909, age-graded lessons were created, triggering a growth spurt in the number and variety of curriculum materials available to churches.

While Baptist churches were involved in the creation of both the secular model and the classic Bible teaching model, they did not invent the concept. The creation of Sunday school (in either form) was quite possibly the greatest ecumenical collaboration in all of history. While Baptists didn't create the model, in the years since the Sunday school began, Baptists have taken the lead in defining and shaping curriculum, literature lines, organization, and growth. Famous Baptist leaders like Arthur Flake, J.N. Barnette, A.V. Washburn, and, in more recent history, Harry Piland, Findley Edge, George Barna, and Leonard Sweet have had a profound impact on the progression of Christian education through the Sunday school. Yet, as involved and committed as Baptists have been in the Sunday school movement, today we are seeing our Sunday school participation numbers decline.

Exactly how did Baptists go from the glory years of the past to today's shrinking state? Did creeping Euro-secularism spread into our society, rendering organized religion culturally out of touch? Perhaps the church failed to note, understand, and act upon the rapidly shifting paradigms that shape and reshape our world? Did this "canonized" tradition that so many churches hold as foundational to their identity and practice lose its relevance for the blooming postmodern generation?

While a case could be made for at least a portion of each possibility, the "canonizing of the tradition" is probably the most likely culprit. "Canonizing" means that we have put the Sunday school to the status of sainthood and have made the program old and staid. The word "tradition" signals the possibility that this program has become old and out of date. The majority of persons attending Sunday school today come because they are expected to or because they always have. Very few come today motivated and excited about the learning experience.

This "canonized tradition" simultaneously represents a precious legacy and a potential curse for churches, especially for the Sunday school. Consider again the origins of the Sunday school concept. Schools were established to teach children the basics of reading, writing, and arithmetic. These programs were modeled after the fledgling secular versions of the day. The secular model saw one teacher, utilizing authoritarian principles, teaching students in classic pedagogical ways. An example of classic pedagogy would be an adult teaching down to a child, with clear lines drawn between teacher and learner.

This model of teaching merged into the framework of the Sunday school as the transition shifted to majoring on religious teaching. With the creation of age-specific literature, these "one-way" teaching methodologies became entrenched. Sadly, many of us in the twenty-first century are still using the approaches formulated in the eighteenth century! While this sounds absurd, it is true that in many cases the same old ways of teaching are still in place. Today many precious learners are being turned off to a vital ministry and meaningful (even life-changing) learning because we have failed to change and adapt.

Take a look at the average Baptist Sunday school class of 1955. Chances are you would find one teacher standing before a small group of students in a small room. That average teacher would lecture for one hour, allowing for a short discussion on world events. And if we flash forward to 1980? Basically the same situation existed in 1980. Unbelievably, this scenario is played out still in churches all over our world today!

Is there anything wrong with this historical sameness? Those who espouse non-traditional or innovative approaches would most likely shout, "Yes!" However, right and wrong should not be the issue in this case. To decry ultra-traditional approaches as wrong will only undermine the critical analysis of the current plight of the majority of struggling Sunday school programs. We would do better to examine the best parts of the ultra-traditional approaches and bring them into our cultural setting of today.

The average adult of 1905 was obviously different than his or her counterpart in 1955. This would also hold true of the average adult of today. This trend of difference continues and will continue as long as the world progresses forward. This is the reason that unchecked or over-revered tradition can (and has) become hurtful to our vitality in the Sunday school.

If the church isn't willing to change and adapt along with society, culture, and the world, then the church will lose her effectiveness as a shaping and influential force in society. The church that holds to the models of 1905 or 1955 out of the misguided belief that tradition is somehow holy or spiritual forfeits the opportunity for making a substantive difference in the world. Jesus warns us about not losing our flavor or our light. Tradition in and of itself is not holy.

Take a glimpse into the modern Sunday school. The most advanced piece of technology likely to be found in most children's Sunday school classes is a flannel board or a faded green chalkboard. In an age of modern print media, most church bulletins today still resemble the layout and design of the 1950s mimeograph. Worship is stagnant in its design and form. Worship still resembles the model of sing, pray, sing, choir special, sermon, pray, sing, go home. Many of us have continued to "do church" the way church was done in the 1950s, often with decreasing results and effectiveness.

We pretend that the majority of Americans are churchgoing Christians who believe in the God of the Bible and who order their lives to reflect this reality. We pretend that the spirituality of Americans in the twenty-first century is enhanced by an outdated diet of practical faith, old-time religion, revivals, and personal "quiet time." We pretend that the church is still the center of community life and that people will come back to church "when they get their lives straightened out." For these reasons, Christianity in general and the ministry of the Sunday school is in deep trouble.[1]

Status Quo or Status Woe

Today's church faces certain tough decisions relating to the future. Researchers today indicate that the average church in America is losing ground in both numerical stability and faith influence. Stephen Carter reports that "two of three adults (67 percent) say they have made a personal commitment to Jesus Christ."[2] Robert Bellah states that "only 41 percent of adults are 'absolutely committed to Christianity' and 44 percent are 'moderately committed'."[3] George Barna adds that while "nine out of ten Americans (88 percent) labeled themselves as 'Christian,' two of three adults had no idea what John 3:16 says and 31 percent could not accurately define 'the gospel'."[4]

Church attendance has also demonstrated a marked decline over the last portion of the twentieth century. From a purely statistical point of view, very few unbelievers are making first-time commitments to Christ as Lord and Savior. Churches seem to be working harder than ever before for fewer and fewer statistical results. Without some kind of positive change, attendance at mainstream churches will probably continue to decline.

Leonard Sweet gives these alarming statistics.[5] Among those aged 18–29, attendance has fallen from 35 percent to 27 percent. Actually, church membership and church-related activities have been declining for 20 years. In 1984, more than 37 percent of people aged 30–39 attended religious services once a week; for their 1995 counterparts, that figure had dropped to 25 percent. Americans may see themselves as churchgoers, but they are not.

And the news just keeps on getting worse. Adult Sunday school attendance continues on the decline. Tome and Joni Shultz have reported that Sunday school participation in mainline denominations declined 55 percent between 1970 and 1990.[6] The total number of churches offering Sunday school during the 1980s declined 43 percent. One out of four adults (23 percent) attended an adult Sunday school class in 1991. The figure had dipped to one out of six (17 percent) in 1996.[7] We are quickly losing an edge that once set us apart. We are failing our culture. We are failing in the Great Commission.

After nearly two decades of studying Christian churches in America, Barna warns convincingly that the typical church as we know it today may soon expire altogether unless we make some drastic changes. He believes that with the present rate of decline, many churches and denominations face extinction.[8]

In the face of these alarming statistics, some researchers are predicting that if present trends continue, sixty percent of all existing Christian congregations in America will disappear before the year 2050! Congregations whose average member is over fifty years of age are especially vulnerable because the average age of Americans is in the mid-thirties and getting younger. Many struggling churches may be forced to close, while others may have to combine with other congregations. Many churches of today may have to restructure and redefine radically their ministries in order to meet the demands of a new day. At the very least, many of us in church today may have to make some changes to reflect a relevance to the world around us.

Hope for the Future? Yes!

With frightening statistics detailing the decline of the modern Protestant church, it does seem fitting and prudent to ask the question "Is there hope for the church?" The answer is an unequivocal "Yes"!

There is hope for the future for most churches, including Baptist churches. However, it will not be easy or necessarily comfortable for the average church to redefine and restructure in order to attract, reach, and assimilate new people.

A minority of churches today, in spite of all the obstacles in place, are redefining their call to ministry. These growing churches reflect a variety of changes brought about by introspection, critical evaluation, prayer, and visionary leadership. There is no singular approach that will work for everyone. However, there are some building blocks that can lead to stopping the flood of decline and maybe even turning the tide around toward growth.

Churches must evaluate with a critical eye the reasons why and how they do church where they are. Local church congregations must decide if growth and renewed vitality is really what they want. If they want to grow and reach people, then the time is now to get serious about doing just that.

As early as 1970, Bruce Larson and Ralph Osborne sounded the alarm.[9] In *The Emerging Church*, the church has been challenged to take *strategy* seriously. From time to time, every church should evaluate and change (or, at least, shift) its strategy according to the surrounding culture, which is definitely changing. However, most churches just keep performing "inherited strategies" that once worked well but now just demand continued support through more budget dollars, more guilt on over-burdened teachers, and more people staying away. Strategy must be developed with a vital vision, a vision that gives shape and direction, integrity and relevance to all that is happening around the church. The vision then leads to appropriate and specific approaches to ministry that will enable the church to achieve its mission in an ever-changing mission field. Very few, if any, mission fields are the same today as they were in 1905, let alone 1955 or even 1985!

Today many churches that were once "out in the country" find themselves swallowed up by suburban sprawl. Many churches that had ample parking and ample space find themselves renting out space to local mission purposes. Many churches that had cutting edge "flannel graph" boards are now trying to figure out how to wire their pre-1950 children's building for computer support. The times are changing!

In order to be successful in a world of increasingly new models, the church must know as much about its field of prospects as possible and then program accordingly. This simple equation is the genesis of success for all growing churches today. Willow Creek Church in suburban Chicago profiles first and then plans for ministries and programs. This approach has also been credited for the enormous success of Saddleback Community Church in Orange County, California.

The Crystal Cathedral in Garden Grove, California, has also been credited to profiling the needs of the community and then programming to meet those needs.

Yes, these are all churches in major metropolitan areas. Yes, these are all churches that have experienced explosive growth recently. And yes, these are all churches that have adopted a variety of innovative methods to reach people. But they have not sacrificed the integrity of the Bible, nor have they ignored their call to be "salt and light" in their communities.

So what is the secret to becoming the next church of explosive growth and cultural relevance? What are some of these "building blocks" to helping the Sunday school regain a position of impact in our communities? We offer the following building blocks not as a prescription for growth but as strategies—an outline—for Sunday school growth. These strategies will work; they have been proven effective. However, each church and each practitioner must take these and "personalize" them for his or her own place of ministry. The following strategies are not a recipe for instant growth. They are a guide for helping churches today customize their Sunday school and grow in relevant and exciting ways to reach more people than ever before with the love of God in Christ.

Building Block 1—Vision

The traditions of the past have been good to us. We have a strong foundation upon which to build and grow. Bless those traditions in your church that are still effective. Embrace those traditions that still have meaning to your congregation. However, do not let tradition hold you captive.

The task of vision is to help us to become who we've been called to be. Vision helps us bless traditions and birth innovations that will help us be more than we already are. Vision pays attention to the major culture shifts in your community. Vision helps you birth innovation. Some innovations can occur by tweaking existing traditions and improving them slightly. Other creative approaches may need a totally new model. Don't be afraid of innovation—birth it, embrace it, and grow!

Building Block 2—Balance in Ministry and Programming

To be truly effective and growing, we must balance the program of Sunday school with the ministry of Sunday school. Too often we focus on one or the other. We end up sacrificing one element or the other at the expense of the total. Sunday school must be balanced in all aspects of programming and ministry to lead to growth and effectiveness.

If we only focus on the programming aspect of the Sunday school, we will have a well-organized and efficient team. If we only focus on programming, we will have a team of teachers, workers, and support staff who are well trained and knowledgeable about the tasks before them. But will anyone be available for *ministry*?

And, if we only focus on the ministry of Sunday school, we will have a people-centered approach to Sunday mornings. If ministry is our priority, we will know everyone in each class and know where everyone is supposed to be. But will we have creative teachers to help us grow deeper in our study of God's word?

Balance is the key to being both organizationally effective and people-centered. Balance will insure that our leadership team is well trained and that the Sunday school cares for all who attend and all who are prospects. Balance will lead us to effective organization and relational ministry.

Building Block 3—Leadership

The Sunday school is the largest single organization in the congregation. The Sunday school has more workers, prospects, and volunteer helpers than any other organization in the congregation. The Sunday school exists for all persons, of all ages, and in all stages of life.

Leadership is crucial for the Sunday school. Sunday school leadership makes sure that the Bible Teaching ministry blends into the other ministries of the church. The Sunday school leadership must remember that Sunday school is not an entity unto itself. The Sunday school reaches, teaches, wins, and develops people in order to support the total ministry of the church.

The Sunday school is to communicate, bring clarity, and support the total work of the church. The Sunday school that exists simply to protect its own ministry will not grow nor be effective. The Sunday school is not an end unto itself. It is the teaching and reaching ministry that leads to church growth. Leaders must make sure that the ministry of the Sunday school stays focused on the total church.

Many today would argue against the effectiveness and importance of the Sunday school. However, as we focus on and support the total work of the church through the Sunday school, we will see excitement, caring relationships, and growth as vital dimensions of our church life. Leadership enables this to happen.

Building Block 4—Relevant and Inspirational Teaching

Relevant and inspiring teaching is the cornerstone of growing through the Sunday school. The Bible is the textbook. The literature is a systematic tool to study the truth of the Scriptures. However, an effective teaching/learning experience is critical to keeping people involved with each other and growing together.

Every person in the world can benefit from the words of the Bible. As we reach and teach people the Bible with relevance and inspiration, lives will be changed. As we impact the lives of those around us, our churches will be transformed and growth will occur. As we grow together and impact people's lives with the truth of Scripture, the world will be changed!

Building Block 5—Outreach and Inreach

We are still in the "people business." Inviting people to participate with us does not mean that all invited will participate. However, we are still called to reach out to those around us. We are called to be intentional about inviting people to share in fellowship, ministry, and learning.

The Sunday school of today must reach out to all in our community. Think about all the people groups that live within a three to five mile circle around your church. Drive through the neighborhoods around your church and strategize ways to make these neighbors aware of your church's ministry. We are called to find, love, and encourage others to join us. And, when they come to us, we are to teach them about God's love.

Building Block 6—Receptivity and Inclusion

We are called to be the body of Christ. We are called to care for the whole world one person at a time. Our Sunday school classes must be on mission to minister to members and prospects. We must even be willing to minister to people who may never join us but who still need the ministry of Christ. Our task is to help them feel comfortable as they come to us. They must feel that we are receptive to them being with us. They must feel that we will make every effort to include them in the life of our church.

Fellowship, caring ministry, and honest relationships will lead us to be effective in our receptivity and inclusion efforts. As we reach people for Sunday school, we do not stop with just reaching and teaching. We minister to others to help them grow and mature in Christ. As we help them grow and mature, they join us in the ministry tasks and strategies of growing our Sunday school.

So What?

The future for all churches and their Sunday schools seems to rest with each individual church. There is hope for a renewed and revitalized future. The first step is with a genuine look at the present and a frank dialogue about how tradition has both helped and hurt the church. Too many of us are asking the wrong questions—"What will make our church grow?" or "Do we want to change?" The right question seems to be, "What values, traditions, programs, leaders are keeping our church from growing?"

Perhaps the best question to begin this journey of blending tradition and innovation may be, "Lord, what would you have us to become?" As we search out the answers to our divine call, maybe we will grow closer to being the church that makes an impact on our culture. As we learn new and innovative ways to share a still relevant message to a constantly changing world, we will make a difference in our Sunday school. The whole world is desperately waiting!

The ways we answer all these questions will go far in determining if churches will live on or fade away. We can choose to continue the decline and risk losing our call to serve God. Or, we can choose to reach people and teach them in the love of Christ. We can choose to ignore the world around us and continue in the same old way doing the same old thing. Or, we can choose to use these building blocks of Sunday school to grow and reach those around us. The choice is yours! Doesn't seem like much of a choice, does it?

Trust God, pray daily, and live on bravely!

Notes

[1] Robert N. Nash, *An 8-Track Church in a CD World* (Macon GA: Smyth & Helwys, 1997), 2.

[2] Stephen L. Carter, *The Culture of Disbelief* (New York: Basic Books, 1993), 41.

[3] Robert Bellah, *Habits of the Heart* (New York: Harper & Row, 1985), 226.

[4]George Barna, *Evangelism That Works* (Ventura CA: Regal Books, 1995), 37.

[5] Leonard Sweet, *Soul Tsunami* (Grand Rapids: Zondervan, 1999), 46.

[6] Tome and Joni Schultz, *Why Nobody Learns Much of Anything at Church* (Loveland, CO: Group, 1993),8.

[7] George Barna, *The Index of Leading Spiritual Leaders* (Nashville: Word, 1996), 1.

[8] George Barna, *The Second Coming of the Church* (Nashville: Word, 1998), 35.

[9] Bruce Larson and Ralph Osborne, *The Emerging Church* (Nashvilile: Word, 1970), 151.

Chapter Two

Building Block 1—Vision

Blessing Tradition/Birthing Innovation

Down one hallway, a small group — although they would never call themselves that — is at its usual Sunday morning work. The Elijah class meets every week for Sunday school, right after morning assembly. A dedicated gathering of old friends, this class has been together for almost forty-eight years. When they formed their class, they created an infrastructure of support, attendance, and prayer as their building blocks. They also agreed to be loyal to the weekly study built around their favorite Sunday school literature. Still today their unwavering adherence to this formula has made them what they are. Despite their age, attendance is strong and they are like family. And they know their Bible fairly well.

Down another hall in the same church, the youngest adult class is having a discussion. Eager to reach other young adults, they are intensely evaluating what their study format should be. They have asked their staff minister to help them brainstorm growth options. They are willing to consider using ongoing literature at least on a half-time basis, but their goal is to stir in some variety. And, of course, they want to approach some topical studies that are "more connected to everyday life."

Week after week, this scenario plays itself out in many churches. Such is the navigational chore for today's Christian educator. Buried somewhere in the job description should be a reference to "directing traffic." In our opening scenario, one group represents tradition — staid and predictable. The other group represents innovation — dynamic and unpredictable. Neither approach by itself is an ideal solution. The need to bless tradition, while addressing an ever-changing spiritual and cultural landscape, is difficult at best. Determining what is sacred and vital versus what is optional and flexible is part of the work that can not be avoided if today's church wants to see tomorrow.

The two groups occasionally stare at each other in disbelief. The older crowd worries about the impetuous nature of the young adults. They forget when they themselves were so willing to risk tradition for growth years ago. They only see the "young folks" willing to abandon the tried and true structure that has made their church the wonderful family that it is now.

The young adults see stubborn inflexibility in the older class. They forget that they themselves are also, in a different way, inflexible and unwilling to compromise. They only see the "gray hairs" as standing in the way of progress and growth that will make the church into an even better church family.

Both groups grow tired of the generational differences that seem to crop up in church life. Both groups see their church as having seen better days. Both groups wonder if their church will ever reclaim a position of influence in the community. Innovation or tradition — which approach to doing church will help these groups return to unity and mission?

Blessing Tradition While Birthing Innovation?

A recent bit of humor brought to light one view of the church's struggle to update. The question is, "How many Baptists does it take to change a light bulb?" The answer is, "Baptists? Change?"!

One pastor of an older, downtown church lamented the realities of holding a mirror up to his congregation. He said that bringing about change in his comfortable, older church was like trying to turn a locomotive with a teaspoon. His analogy highlights the emotional drain of trying to take on the mammoth transitional tasks involved.

What does it mean to birth innovation? Simply put, today's carefully guarded traditions had to come from somewhere. While some of them seemed to evolve inexplicably, others were conscious efforts to address needs of some type. Many church ideas that have become old and reliable were created as growth strategies from visionary leadership. While respecting and accommodating the very best of our traditions, we must be about the task of birthing tomorrow's new forms. Though some of these will fail or function only for short times, many of them will survive and thrive. They will have been birthed and blessed in the shadow of those seeming non-negotiables that came before.

One of the largest summer youth camps of our time was an idea that was first jotted down on a scrap of paper, only to be deemed pointless and not feasible. Filed away in a cabinet for years, a need eventually arose that called for innovation. The scrap of paper was retrieved and the concept fleshed out. Two decades later, the program is now firmly etched into the fabric of summer activity. Little did anyone know at the time that a tradition was being birthed out of church need.

This illustration calls us back for another look at our two Sunday school groups. If you can get the right senior adults to share, they can tell you about a remarkable episode in their church's history. When the present senior adults were young, the old leaders of the church failed to make room for them. So, forty years ago, some brash thirtysomethings called a meeting and confronted the power structure. Wealthy and accustomed to getting their way, the older deacons and committee chairs bristled at first. Then, they slowly realized that the youngsters might have a point. Church leadership circles opened somewhat, and an uneasy transition was begun. Now, those brash youngsters, grown old, have somehow claimed the seats of inflexibility their forebears occupied. The Elijah class is no longer the hotbed of visionary ideology. The class's natural mode is now to preserve the familiar. And, today's young adults pushing their own envelopes will most likely follow in the same cycle.

There are some basic assumptions involved in believing that a church can be successful in a move toward a viable future. These general assumptions that follow represent values and practices that must be called on in great measure for the developing congregation. They are also based on a strong vision of who the church is and who God is calling us to become.

• *A congregation that is able to dialogue.* There will need to be honest conversation on many levels. Efforts will have to facilitate the healthy goal of doing kingdom work. Trying to define just what that kingdom work is for the congregation may be complicated at times. Growing an understanding and respect between multiple generations will not happen without high levels of vision, communication, and prayer.

• *A congregation that is a literate church.* Where its view of Scripture and theology is concerned, the congregation understands who they are. Drawing from functional models of congregational life, a body of believers will have to find common ground upon which to make decisions. Congregational government and worship practice will both be crucial to effective body life.

• *A congregation that is a healthy church.* A healthy church is built around the trust of fellow members. A general air of cynicism and disbelief cripples most visionary efforts before they ever have a chance. Distrust and shortsightedness frustrates most visionary leaders. A healthy church supports a creative atmosphere of vision and interaction. Relationships within the body are guarded and supported. The friendships within the body take precedence over the traditions of the institution.

• *A congregation that has an appropriate "mission."* This mission is not a task only done somewhere "out there." Today, long range planning for most corporate groups is eighteen months to three years. The church of tomorrow will have to accept that the persons within a one-mile, five-mile, or ten-mile radius (and more?) of the church's doors are worthy of entrepreneurial effort. These attitudes and techniques have been historically entrusted to mission boards and agencies. Other groups previously set the agenda for our churches. No more!

Missions will now have to be embraced by the local church as well. Every visionary church into the future may have to include strategizing for specialized outreach and ministry. Previously, open doors and a church sign have been enough. New points of entry will have to be discovered and developed. The church of today must embrace the new status of a valid mission outpost.

• *A congregation that can translate their values, beliefs, and vision into action.* The gathered community of believers must be able to put their theology into practice. The value of an exciting vision is in the execution of the vision by the group. The only way a community of faith can reliably act on its collective conscience is for its members to act on their faith in their individual daily lives. This delicate issue is, unfortunately, a most difficult ideal to achieve.

• *A congregation that can be informed by the culture without being unduly shaped by the culture.* While some forms and practices should be flexible, our culture reinvents itself far too rapidly for the church to sell out completely to fads and trends. The church will have to make its decisions wisely. There is a fine line between a creative visionary and a ranting lunatic. We must continually pray the prayer of St. Francis for serenity and vision and wise choices.

Cultural Tail-Chasing?

Some churches do not struggle as deeply with the bindings of tradition. Many congregations have decided to make wholesale changes in attempt to bring about some type of last-minute comeback. In each case, these profiles are usually based on their interpretation of current societal trends. Trouble is, American culture is now said to reinvent itself about once every three to five years. If our joke about Baptists and change is informative at all, then the average church is at least slower than most corporate settings. Churches are usually ten to twenty years behind cultural norms. Most church persons speaking about "tomorrow" are likely talking about today or, even more likely, yesterday!

Ever watch a puppy chase its tail? You can find yourself mesmerized by this comical sight. At some point, you feel a little sorry for the dog, since your human reasoning has surmised that the poor dog will probably never catch the tail. This is the trap into which many modern churches can fall. These "cultural tail-chasers" jump at every church guru prediction only to find themselves dizzy and with blurred vision. A clear vision keeps us from tail-chasing and lets us stay focused on our true mission. This saves us from wasting the energy of our leaders, from frivolous spending of ministry dollars, and from making other costly mistakes.

True, our notions and practices cannot be devoid of cultural influence. In fact, we must be aware of and informed by our culture. If we are to understand people, ourselves included, then the church must live at some level of peace within its culture. The chore is to make wise decisions as to how our cultural and demographic decisions will influence our values, structures, and programs as a church community. There will have to be a delicate blending of non-negotiables and pockets of flexibility. This is easier to write about than it is to practice. But still, we must keep praying for vision and flexibility, for unity and understanding. And we must live out God's call as best we can!

An Example from Church Life

One of the most frequently observed arenas for church change is worship. Based on a perceived cultural mandate, many churches have rushed to a seat in the debate about worship styles. Many of our congregations have opted to offer alternative or contemporary worship services. A few years ago, the number of ministerial dialogues about how to create and manage these services was staggering. Now, it seems that one is just as likely to hear a conversation about how to terminate a contemporary service as to hear about one being implemented. Why the turnaround?

One answer to the dilemma is shared from culture. The same young adults who demanded the new formats are now moving on to an interest in more traditional, liturgical styles of worship. The telling quote by one young adult: "I've done the contemporary thing. It was fun. Now I'm ready to go back to church."

Is this an indictment against contemporary worship? No, this is more a commentary on the process of change. Many churches may have found peace with newer worship formats and discovered viable ways of reaching potential churchgoers in their locales. But others simply created another time slot in which their people could attend worship and get home an hour earlier.

The same can be said for how Christian education is packaged and offered in our churches. For worship, education, community-building, and missions, our grounding must be far more central than our forms. We simply have to begin church study and dialogue on biblical and personal (local) values that will serve us for a much longer period of time. Then, informed to a degree by our culture, we can shape our programmatic styles. When our decisions are based on roots deeper than mere cultural/demographic studies alone, we are able to meet persons where they are while retaining our own personal and corporate sense of spiritual integrity.

There is no cookie-cutter way to do worship or Christian education. Though some groups give prescriptive advice, most of us edit their advice to fit our situations. And well we should! Most ministry techniques will be sensitive to their community settings. The forms and techniques must have support of the people in order to work. In a spiritual democracy, there is a common misconception that the people of God will always know what they need. We mistake our "majority rule" customs for constant or infallible guidance in matters of faith. Healthy kingdom leadership brings about a consensus informed by the will of church members, but inspired by true spiritual vision. God's people must be on board with any direction that is to be successful. But those who have a feel for the long-term greater good must lead them.

Traditions are Former Innovations That Have Been Transformed!

Funny how innovations stick around to become staid traditions. Some even get written into bylaws and policies. Others become such legendary oral traditions that they wind up being recorded on paper in spite of not being officially voted upon. Soon, an organization is protecting these aging practices as though they are to stand forever. Former innovations have been transformed into immovable traditions.

A healthy organization finds a way to honor traditions while birthing new ones. Visionary leadership is the key! There is no reason to clean house of the old ways just for recreational or rebellious motivation. With honest dialogue and a great deal of patience from all parties, a group can discern the absolutes from the options. Vision helps us attain the balance necessary to maintain our fellowship while transforming.

Like a corporation with true entrepreneurial ability, the church must create an atmosphere that spawns needed change while honoring necessary customs. No family or friendship ever clips along without an occasional bump in the road. The give and take of relationships will have to be exposed to the political and evaluative processes that have been put into place. Sometimes, change even works in reverse, causing an organization to discover new ways to make decisions along the journey to new eras. The important point to remember is that we stay dynamic in our thinking and practice. When we embrace an innovation as the end-all of our practice, then tradition sets in and we grow stagnant once again.

All Things to All People?

Churches have personalities and gifts, and they're waiting to be discovered. Sometimes, getting a clear feel for who we are as collective bodies is tough. We put into place structures and habits that will carefully guard against ever discovering anything new. Meanwhile, the individuals making up the group have come and gone. A new family joins here, a funeral is done there, and a new person visiting regularly is added to the mix. Soon, there can be a different feel. But be careful. That group may not be as new as it appears.

A city in the southeast has about half a million people in the metropolitan area. True to its Bible Belt surroundings, there are some 450 churches located within one county of the metropolitan area alone. An astonishing variety of faith groups are represented and all the traditional mainline groups are also there. One historical congregation has created 18 mission churches alone!

Still, the reality is that no person could likely be comfortable in all 450 of the available churches there. There is a good reason for most of the groups existing in this demographic area. They represent an array of theological stances and worship practices. They are made up of individuals from all across the economic and social strata. Some smaller bodies serve tight geographic pockets, while some larger ones may draw from the entire region. Suddenly, one realizes that few of the churches are actually alike. Even with the diminishing emphasis on denominations, these churches are distinct from each other in belief and practice.

While the generations may come and go, these bodies take on individual personalities, too. They develop patterns of decision-making and planning. They take on a language and an inner culture. They differ in the types of ministry emphases that excite them. A surprise awaits the person who moves from one city to another. The large church of his preference in a former city may not resemble the one that awaits him in his next town.

We have to be honest about a few basic notions:

• *What one church is good at, another may not be able to do well at all.* Some congregations are great at hospitality and spiritual nurture. Others are stronger at worship. Still others are gifted in pastoral care and hands-on missions. Likely, they are not as good as they think they are at all they do. One wise sage said, "I don't understand all I know."

• *Individual, personal agendas make it tough to get a true picture of a body's collective giftedness.* Sometimes, that personal agenda is genuine conviction about ministry direction. Still, hard decisions have to be made under the collective leadership of the spirit.

• *A church can be all things to all people.* In fact, most of the time, this type of belief leads to a watering down of church gifts and missions needs. To believe that a body can be of ultimate use to the Kingdom, in more than just a few basic areas of service, is to border on spiritual arrogance.

• *We are what we used to be.* While churches have personalities, they can shift over time. An outsider can take a personality "snapshot" and get a picture of who a gathered body is today. But, the church might not recognize its own portrait. Holding on to the old for no true reason can rob us of the chance to take on the new.

Just as persons cannot assume than just any church will be the right fit to practice their faith, churches have to be real about their identities too. Like an individual, a church has to get comfortable with whom God has gifted them to be. This means accepting limitations and discovering strengths that may as yet lie completely misunderstood. This means becoming ready to grasp God's vision and to carry it like a torch along the way.

Biblical Health and Community

What is biblical health? That is a fair question. The answer, however, is not so easy. The first place to search for an answer is in a familiar passage of Scripture. One might find an image of community like the one recorded in Acts 2 and seek to implement its practices to the letter. Worship practices could be taken literally from any number of the Psalms. Church leadership structure could be gained from Paul's writings or those found again in Acts. Old Testament specifications for buildings and decision-making abound.

Sadly, there are no cookie-cutter patterns for today's church in Scripture. There are enough differences in form and structure within our Bible that cases and counter cases can be made to support just about anything. Our reality is that the kingdom effort will involve a little more study and discernment than any one person can do alone.

Congregations will have to become more biblically literate in order to develop an overall sense of God's movement in their midst. They will have to invest in quality instruction, both in terms of time and resources. They will have to seek an honest willingness to give dialogue to the complexities of being church today.

What are some biblical health checkpoints for churches doing visionary kingdom work?

- *A commitment to balanced study in theology, history, ethics, missions, Scripture, and spiritual disciplines.* Whatever a congregation's road map is to look like, its leadership will have to be rooted in sincere and fresh discovery of these age-old basics. These can be done in fresh and exciting ways. They do not have to be called by these rather bland names. But they will have to be there.

- *The handling of God's Scripture must be done humbly and with education.* The Bible cannot be wielded as a weapon of manipulation. We can take Bible verses out of context and twist the meanings to fit our agenda. We can also use Scripture to bring unity to those who prayerfully educate themselves and genuinely seek its direction.

- *All operations and movements of the church will have to be conducted with the highest ethical standards.* This means that truth and integrity, long assumed to be "givens" in churches, will have to be restored where they are lacking. When, and if, they can be restored.

- *Godward worship and study will have to be practiced in order to have biblical health.* Many church practices and services feature humans as the center. They are designed to "feed" those who attend. What we do will have to be of top quality today. For better or worse, our churches are compared to the top concerts, ballgames, television shows, and movies. The reality is that we can never measure up to these comparisons. We have neither budgets nor expertise to be another purely entertainment venue. Worship centers on God first and foremost. Our entertainment and fun is a side benefit of a good church experience, not the centerpiece.

• *"Sit-and-soak church" creates lazy Christians over the long-term.* The Bible is about an active faith. The Bible engages its believers and empowers them to go out and do. We are compelled to serve more than to be served. A biblically healthy church spins believers out to make better homes and neighborhoods.

Function Over Form

A final challenge for churches will be to separate form from function. This will apply no more strongly in churches than in the areas of Christian education and worship. The difference between the terms is night and day. Yet, we struggle as collections of individuals to get on the same page.

Will the church teach? The church will have to in the days to come. But what it teaches and how it teaches are separated by form and function. Until those definitions are understood in common, getting down to healthy evaluation and decision-making is difficult at best.

Function might be quickly understood as the goals of the teaching. For instance, a church might decide that it wants to invest in better biblical knowledge and mission awareness over the next two years. It will use a variety of programs or events to accomplish that improved teaching. That will be its goal or function. All action plans designed or identified to accomplish that goal speak to function.

Form has to do with how the church will accomplish that teaching. This is where the wonderful but confusing variety of approaches comes in. There are endless forms that we can use. Don't limit the creativity of your minds or the leadership of the Holy Spirit in developing endless approaches to exciting worship and learning experiences.

One church struggles to convert its age-old mission groupings to newer forms that will help ensure active participation for the future. While one faction tends to enjoy monthly meals with guest speakers and financial offerings, another generation wishes to get out and do various hands-on projects in the community. Their monetary giving is directly affected by their past experiences with having done actual mission efforts. Both approaches serve the *function* of teaching about missions. Their *forms* differ greatly, though.

The dialogue will have to be clarified with regard to form and function. Arguments often ensue because parties are lobbying for form while forgetting the ultimate goal, or function. Sometimes, there is room for more than one form, allowing for more participants to benefit from the ministry goal. Compromise can be reached when multiple visions can be accommodated within a healthy program. Keep in mind that a group can be a poor steward of energy and interest when trying to use too many forms. There are often hard decisions to be made, and they will test the trust and communication of a body. Compromise has its limits.

Issues surrounding the blessing of tradition and birthing of innovation are easily discussed. Admittedly, they are tricky to practice. They should be dealt with nonetheless. There is no progress in ignoring the complexities of corporate spiritual life. To be sure, latent congregational issues will surface at some time. Left to their own timing, they usually surface at all the wrong crossroads. The proactive congregation deals with them as an intentional part of casting vision when at all possible.

So What?

Vision is the building block upon which all the others rest. Forging an atmosphere of healthy visioning surrounds our efforts with a chance to be useful to God. That's our common call. This is a call that brings unity and health to the body. This is a call that maximizes our efforts and minimizes our divisions. This is a call that gives energy and produces a legacy of resulting tradition and innovation.

As we dream great dreams for God, we will attempt great things for God. Vision gives us direction and purpose. Vision keeps us focused on our individual and common calls. This is a call that ultimately brings blessings and, if we're lucky, miracles.

Trust God, pray daily, and live on bravely!

Chapter Three

Building Block 2—Balance

"Let's Take Marty, for Example . . . "

"He's been here in this church his whole life." So the education team brainstorming began. An attempt to rethink the church's Christian education plan was underway with a practical example. Everyone at the table knew Marty. Although it would be narrowly focused to evaluate the whole Bible teaching ministry based on one person's needs, he would be a good representative of a larger group. The brainstorming continued . . . .

"His parents were key participants and did a lot of good for the congregation. They raised him in the faith, and he's reached retirement age now. Marty sings in three choirs and has served on every leadership group we have. He's just buried his dad. He's comfortable at work and in the community. Marty will probably be here for the rest of his life.

"What does he need in the way of spiritual formation that the church can provide? Through what passages have we walked with him as he has lived? Silly as it might sound, let's pretend that we can be the education team for his whole life."

Like a contractor building a house, this team worked to discover a blueprint with which to proceed. In that first meeting, their real issues included:

• What do we mean by "Christian education"? What are we talking about?
• Are there some basic elements to spiritual growth that ought to be "taught" through a combination of programmed and non-programmed efforts?
• Will these basics be subject to cultural changes over the years, or will they be more enduring?
• What strengths and resources are at our disposal in the attempt to provide meaningful spiritual nurture?
• What limitations do we face? What are our weaknesses in providing meaningful spiritual nurture?

Questions like these are decent starting points in the journey toward balanced, intentional, education planning. There are few ready-made answers to the above core questions. However, any church would do well to search for some of the answers. A church's biases, faith/worship styles, and perceived resources will color the answers in great part. Those answers will be important in determining what is actually done. And many of the answers and anticipated outcomes will lean heavily upon the quality of ministry through the Sunday school.

In the workbook "Blueprints," the Cooperative Baptist Fellowship has attempted to provide a framework around which to brainstorm these issues. Building around what are referred to as *vertical* and *horizontal* relationships, a church should try to find balance in its programming approaches. The vertical plane of relationships examines the interaction of humans with God. The horizontal plane deals with interpersonal relationships between persons. This is how well each of us relates to the rest of us. In using this tool as a basis for planning, the Sunday school will emerge with a balanced approach to ministry, Bible teaching, outreach, and fellowship.

Where Does the Sunday School Fit In?

Clearly, the Sunday school cannot be the extent of a church's efforts to nurture and discipleship. Yet, so many churches don't program much else. The Sunday school was never intended to be the church's only program of consistent Bible study. The Sunday school was also not designed to provide "in-depth" Bible study. The Sunday school provides opportunities for reaching, teaching, developing, and discipling. There is not time for "in-depth" study. There must be more!

The Sunday school can offer multiple tracks of study happening in that hour of study each week. Each study is biblically-based, but some of these tracks are "elective" Bible book studies or topical studies. There are many needs to be met.

There are macro or "big picture" results that can be accomplished. The congregation studies the Bible, the congregation grows in understanding of biblical truths. These macro needs are what applies to the congregation or even the church's community as a whole. There are also micro or "little picture" results that can be accomplished in a healthy environment of learning. These can be as diverse as what is happening in each of the age groups of study to what is happening in the life of each person attending that day.

The Sunday school is the largest single gathering of people each week. There must be a realistic and creative understanding of all that can be accomplished in the Bible teaching hour. There must be a communication of realistic expectations of what *can* happen during the hour. There must be balance!

In the macro or large picture sense, Sunday school yields a breadth of wonderful outcomes for the church. Among these, it facilitates:

- *Bible Study* that builds a basic familiarity with the Scripture. This will build a basis for all other elements of the church's life, including worship, discipleship, and missions.
- *Outreach* on behalf of the larger body. Although more people now enter the doors of our churches through worship and fellowship, small group Bible study still helps to assimilate them in a special way. These gatherings are among the smaller groupings that let people build relationships.
- *Fellowship* that can give a healthy sense of community. The typical worship or churchwide gathering cannot give the intimacy that sustains participation over the long haul. Small gatherings can provide this dynamic.

• *Pastoral care* that is shared back and forth as group or class members have need. Celebration in good times and support in tougher times is a priceless result of trusting relationships.
• *Encouragement and interpretation* of the church's larger community. There is much to be gained when the smaller groups encourage participation back to the larger body.
• *Practice of basic spiritual disciplines.* There are many good resources to help us gain an understanding of some basic elements of growth. These can be built in to the life of the class as "homework" assignments, for example. Or, the class might choose to go outside the literature for a short-term study of a resource.

In the micro sense, the Bible teaching ministry is a vehicle that can move toward small doses of a church's core curriculum. These basics should pervade all arenas in the church's life. While learning Bible stories and facts, these lessons also make a concentrated effort to teach:

• *theology and doctrine,* which undergird life's values and decision-making. This is a vital support system for the worshipping church, and a center around which all else is drawn.
• *church history,* from which we must learn or be doomed to repeat the mistakes of the past. And, without an understanding of this history, we are in danger of missing out on the blessings of the future!
• *spirituality,* in which the shared responsibility of growth enriches the journey. Healthy study habits contribute to the practice of spiritual disciplines.
• *mission,* which gives opportunity to turn compassion into action.
• *ethics,* one of the results of a life lived in tune with God's leading. Sunday school should produce Christians whose lives pulse with testimony to their values.

The exposure to these core elements will not substitute for other opportunities to teach and disciple in more focused ways. These elements only provide a good starting point for the building of the church. And, delivered in the context of a weekly gathering, they stand a strong chance of sowing good seeds along the way. Our task is to find balance between the "macro" and "micro" elements to insure an intentional and focused ministry approach.

Nothing Never Happens!

In another chapter, teaching and learning styles are discussed. But a quick tour of most church facilities will show whether the church is providing an interactive, living laboratory where balanced Christian growth takes place. Rooms with rows of chairs aimed toward a lectern cast doubt on a participatory or shared experience. A circle lends hope that members are being facilitated toward a sharing of their lives. Conference rooms provide a place of learning, as well as sanctuaries and fellowship place. Space where mission activity can be prepared speaks to health as well.

Viewed from an even broader perspective, one should see the church building as a place where "nothing never happens." Christian educator and pastor John Hendrix coined this phrase decades ago. His point is that God's people are constantly educating the people around them. Through their attitudes, their actions, and their biases, they are educating each other. The message communicated is either positive or negative, but the education takes place all the same.

A Real Life Example

Consider the church member who teaches in the children's Sunday school. She faithfully volunteers in the third grade area as a Bible story teacher. She also is the third grade teacher in the local elementary school, where her reputation for abusive treatment of children was legendary. She communicates to most everyone that God's people can be both pious and destructive all at the same time.

In contrast, the wealthiest gentleman in that same church is also a Sunday school teacher. On a scale where wealth and power carried tremendous status, he was certainly near the top of the status scale. Yet, he is known to be perhaps the friendliest and most dedicated member of the church. He displays humility in his growing faith. He models that God's people can live on a higher plain, resisting piety and abusive behavior. His status does not get in the way of his faith.

In different ways, these two people exemplified the powerful reality that "nothing never happens; something always happens." Wherever we go and whatever we might be doing, people notice. No matter how we behave, people notice. In every situation, *something* still happens! We either are a missionary or a mission field. We either are a positive witness for Christ or a negative one. But "nothing" never happens!

One Church—Multiple Tracks

It is vital to understand that there are a multitude of small miracles happening each week in Sunday school. A prepared teacher who involves and loves the class members teaches something much larger than the day's prescribed lesson. She or he teaches that the growth of God's people is a valuable goal to pursue. The teacher also communicates care for his/her class. A tardy volunteer who is unreliable teaches something altogether different. Likewise, a program design that reflects a sense of investment through balance teaches more than the sum of its elements.

In her book *Fashion Me A People*, Maria Harris calls our attention to three curricula of the church.[1] Paying attention to our teaching approaches again helps us strive for balance.

The *explicit curriculum* refers to what is actually presented in a teaching effort. The explicit is the things we say and the things we do. A Sunday school lesson from a study guide, a lesson plan, or a literature piece shapes our approach to a given Scripture lesson. The lesson has a goal of teaching some basic concept or belief. The explicit curriculum is the stated goal of the lesson and all the approaches we use to convey the lesson.

The *implicit curriculum* refers to the structures in place to facilitate the program. The implicit is the things underlying the things we say and do. Ranging from organizational efforts to facilities, and from traditions to processes, these elements influence how the teaching will be carried out. The implicit includes our biases, values, and comfort zones. The implicit includes what we *mean* by what we say and do. This curriculum ends up shaping or determining how the explicit is understood. And, this can add elements to the explicit that were not planned. For instance, if a statement or learning approach is misunderstood, the teaching plan may be interrupted to explain more clearly why something was said or done.

The *null curriculum,* according to Harris, consists of all that is left out. The null is all that we don't say and do and the meaning behind these. She emphasizes that the ignorance of or the absence of something is not neutral. That which we do not facilitate or provide for is also a teaching element of the church. When we play to our strengths and ignore blind spots, we stir in the null curricula. The null is a shaper of our efforts, including the atmosphere in which we do Sunday school. Remember, nothing *never* happens. Everything has meaning. Something always happens!

The Sunday school has an opportunity to be central in the educational efforts of the church. The Sunday school models healthy learning and healthy community. The Sunday school produces leaders for itself and other church ministries. The Sunday school brings balance to a church's ministry of reaching, teaching, developing, and discipling.

Not all of the church's efforts to teach will be as programmed as the Sunday school, nor should they be. Many of the greatest teaching opportunities will arise during informal gatherings. Still, to harness the unlimited power of the Sunday school is to posture the church for health. An understanding of its place in the larger scheme is the start to evaluating your church's effort. This understanding will lead to a balanced approach of Proclamation, Education, Fellowship, Service, Prayer, and Worship!

So What?

Balance is what keeps us poised and stabilized and able to do quality ministry. Balance helps us keep the people in the congregation, the ministries of the church, the spiritual and material resources, and the administrative procedures of the church in equilibrium. This balancing act sometimes resembles a constant state of motion and chaos, somewhat like the old vaudeville actor spinning plates! Balance does not come easy. This building block will help bring some simplicity to the complexity of this postmodern world with which we find ourselves wrestling. Growth demands balance.

Trust God, pray daily, and live on bravely!

Note

[1] Maria Harris, *Fashion Me A People: Curriculum in the Church* (Louisville: Westminster/John Knox Press, 1989), 68-70.

Chapter Four

Building Block 3–Leadership

The Church Resembles the Church Staff

This statement bears out the critical stance of positive and effective Sunday school leadership. If the church of today is going to grow, leadership will play a vital role in growing the organization. The average church has about 100 to 150 in total attendance each week. One hundred people demand attention and leadership. Although many churches will be larger than 100 in attendance (and some smaller too), leadership is called to support and sustain the work and ministry of the church.

The staff has a huge responsibility to lead the church. We cannot do ministry by ourselves. We need one another to grow a successful ministry. The level at which the staff is motivated, dedicated, and forward thinking will determine the level at which the church will function as well. But the church staff or the pastor alone is not called to meet *every* need in the church. The staff ministers are called to make sure that all the needs are being met!

So how do church staffs operate at high levels of quality and dedication? What needs to happen for leadership to form into a quality functioning team? These are complex questions and so are the answers. The staff is to share ministry in both the sorrows and the joys of their congregation. The staff is to reach, teach, minister, and equip. The staff is to pull in the same direction, working toward the same goals. The staff is to be a team of leaders. And that's where the leadership of the Sunday school comes into play. The Sunday school leadership is also called to be a team!

TEAM—Together Everyone Accomplishes More

Good teams function together as one unit. The leadership team members cover for one another, share in the joys, and support in the frustrations. The leadership team of the Sunday school is sometimes referred to as the Christian Education Council, the Sunday School Council, or the Education Committee. Regardless of what you call this group, their work will only be as effective as their ability to be a team of servant leaders.

The Sunday school leadership team is made up of everyone who has leadership responsibilities in the administration of the Sunday school. Usually, the staff minister (or staff ministers in charge of Sunday school leadership) direct the work of the leadership team. The minister works closely with the officers of the Sunday school; these may include the Sunday school director, the Sunday school outreach director, and the Sunday school training director. In addition, if the church uses directors to help with age group divisions, these should also be included. If there are other officers in the Sunday school, they should also be included in the leadership team.

If the church doesn't have a large Sunday school organization, consider inviting the teachers to be a part of this team. In a larger church setting, limit the participants to those who have direct responsibility for the administration of the total Sunday school ministry. Not including enough leaders or including too many will both be counterproductive. Include and involve only those who are directly involved in helping lead the Sunday school.

However, the people serving on the council and the name of the group are mute points if the group does not form a strong team. Team ministry means that you share, communicate, unite, and dedicate yourselves toward the successful accomplishment of common goals. Teamwork is difficult work. The elements below must be present in some form if you are going to be a successful team.

• *Loyalty.* We will only be as successful in our individual ministries as the team is successful in its combined ministry! Loyalty to one another is crucial. Public conflict between staff members is crippling. Communication among team members builds loyalty. There will always be Sunday school teachers and leaders who want to gripe and complain. Some of these people will try to divide and conquer the leadership team.

We once had a teacher who would go to every one of the Sunday School Council members until she got a "yes" answer to her question. She knew how to manipulate us against each other. We soon learned that clear communication among all of us was a *must.* Soon, we became a tightly knit group aware of the ways of those who wanted their own way.

• *Competence.* Sunday morning is the main priority of the Sunday school leadership team. Make sure you prepare adequately each week to allow your team to be confident in the Sunday morning responsibilities. The competent Sunday school leadership team makes sure that rooms are ready, that teachers' needs are met, and that everything is in place to support a quality Bible teaching ministry. While there may be some touchy situations in which you will be called on to lead, *never* let them see you sweat!

• *Focus.* The quality and competent Sunday school leadership team makes sure that they are focused on the right priorities. Too many leaders focus just on doing things the right way. They are only concerned with the procedures of how things are done. These leaders focus on tradition and policy. These leaders probably focus too much on approach. If not careful, these defenders of tradition will lose their focus and become obstacles for growth.

There are other leaders who focus all of their energy on doing the right things. These leaders appear visionary. They keep us focused on meeting the needs of our community and keep us dreaming great dreams. If left unchecked, however, these vision casters will get too far out in front of the rest of the team. They will lose their effectiveness because they will be looked upon as too wild and too weird.

Effective leadership balances vision and procedure. We must dream great dreams. We must pay attention to the details. Only a focused leadership team can make sure that we stay balanced in the leadership we provide our teachers.

• *Leadership Development.* Much of the leadership literature of today talks about the leader continuing to develop followers. The leader who can develop a strong group of followers will be in a position to get things done. Leaders who develop followers will be inspirational and motivational. Leaders who can develop followers will be able to challenge others and to bring about the changes that he/she desires. The leader who develops followers will always have a strong group of supporters willing to "make it happen."

However, there is another approach that can be just as effective. Good leaders develop other "good leaders." Leaders involved in developing good leaders are not just using personality and motivation. The development of other leaders is a must if the organization is going to grow. By multiplying one's talents and leadership abilities, the organization will grow beyond the inspiration and motivation of just one leader.

The leader who develops other leaders also ensures a strong base of support. This leader is also motivational and inspirational. But this leader also makes sure that there will be leaders to "fill the gaps" when other leaders are needed.

We must make every effort through our own leadership to build a team of leaders that will guide our Sunday school. As we build team members, we build a group of flexible and energized people willing to put the needs of others before their own needs. Successful Sunday school leadership teams have an agreed upon mission. Successful Sunday school leadership teams have an unselfishness of work and ministry tasks. Successful Sunday school leadership teams have a high level of competence and unity.

We have good leaders right now, but we will need more! Leadership development will be a key in the coming years. Teachers will always be needed . . . but so are other leaders in the class and in the organization. The sign of an effective teacher is both how many people they keep *in* their class and how many people they send *out* of their class.

Servant Leadership

Servant-leadership is a philosophy developed by Robert Greenleaf in the late 1960s. Greenleaf described servant-leadership in his groundbreaking book, *The Servant as Leader* in 1970.[1] The servant-leader is one who strives to serve. The servant-leader makes a conscious choice to aspire to lead. The servant-leader makes sure that other people's highest priority needs are being served first and then takes care of his/her own needs.

Many a minister/leader has heard the "servanthood" drill. We have been challenged to "give 'til it hurts" and "to give unselfishly." This model of servanthood is known more as that of "suffering servant" or even "suffering slave"! That is not the model Greenleaf proposed.

Servant-leadership puts people first in order to help them grow and develop. Servant-leadership attempts to enhance the personal growth of workers and improve the quality and caring environment of the organization. This style of leadership involves a combination of teamwork, community building, personal involvement in decision-making, and ethical behavior.

Servant-leadership is built upon a covenant relationship between leadership and follower-ship. The servant-leader takes time to listen, shares empathy, seeks to be an instrument of healing, is a good steward of time and resources, and is committed to helping others grow both personally and in the context of community. Servant-leadership communicates a caring and intentional relationship with the congregation.

Servant-leadership does away with typical authoritative and hierarchical organization. Servant-leadership stresses collaboration, teamwork, and mutual respect between team members, the organization, and the congregation. This approach to leadership requires a high degree of professional respect for the gifts and abilities of staff colleagues. The "Lone Ranger" minister doing all things for all people or the "Godfather" pastor giving orders and bossing others will not be very effective as a leader in today's postmodern church.

The servant-leader is committed to growing everyone in the organization, whether a follower or another leader. The servant-leader takes great care to put others first and self last.

The Ten Commandments for Leadership Teams

(1) *Dream big.* What do you want your Sunday school to become? Spend time in retreat, prayer, and study, asking God's guidance. As God directs, gather a sense of how you are to work and move forward in faith. Too often we are just content to maintain the status quo. This building block of leadership for Sunday school growth is not content to maintain "the way we've always done it before." Where there is no vision, the people perish. Where there is a little vision, the people become bored! There is nothing worse than a bored congregation (see Rev 3:14-16). Dare to dream so big and bold that you are destined to fail without God's intervention. Be realistic, be pragmatic, but be filled with a dream worthy of God's partnership with us.

(2) *Balance people and purpose.* Too often, leaders are only interested in taking care of the tasks. The tasks are important; there is much to do every week. However, too much emphasis on the tasks may take us away from a sensitivity to ministry. If we focus too heavily on what needs to be done, we may overlook significant opportunities for ministry and fellowship. Too often, leaders are only interested in meeting the needs of the people. The people are important; there are many needs that must be met each week. However, too much emphasis on ministry needs may take us away from an attention to action. If we focus too heavily on the ministry needs of people, we may overlook significant activities for supporting the work each week.

(3) *Respond quickly to church guests and prospects.* Part of the impression we make on those who visit our church is based on how we respond to them *after* they leave. A call or card to all who visit each week speaks volumes about how much we care for the unchurched

and prospects. Most churches in a plateaued or decreasing situation are not interested in evangelism or even hospitality. Growing churches take the initiative to make members, prospective members, and church guests feel welcomed. As we contact quickly, we communicate that we care. We will not have everyone who visits join our church or attend our Sunday school, but we will have an opportunity to minister to all whom we contact. Growth rarely comes when we ignore others. Growth usually happens when we pay attention to the needs to others.

(4) *Remember that staff is important.* One person cannot adequately minister to more than 100 people. Church growth specialists emphasize the importance of expanding the ministry staff to respond to growing congregations. The ministry staff is charged with equipping the membership. The ministry staff is charged with leading in outreach and inreach. If leaders are spread too thin, they quickly become ineffective and inattentive. Burnout is quick to occur. Just as we must provide adequate staff ministers for the congregation, we must also allow adequate lay leadership. The ratio for volunteer leadership is one leader for every 25–50 people. The volunteer leader will not have a dedicated amount of time to invest. The Sunday school teacher will not have an overabundance of time for leading a class. Assigning the Sunday school leadership team to care for too many people discourages their leadership.

When we program with adequate professional staff and volunteer leaders, we allow each minister and volunteer leader to lead from their strengths and stay energized. As we keep leaders energized, enthused, and motivated, their effectiveness, creativity, and length of service increases. As tenure increases, ministry abounds through trust, vision, and deeper relationships.

(5) *Empower others to do their work.* There is nothing more defeating than a leader who will not share. As we enlist others to work with us, we must give them the opportunity and the authority to make decisions. As we empower others, we communicate trust and confidence in their leadership. Empowerment may mean that you give resources,

materials, and opportunities for others to lead. Empowerment may mean that we move out of the way and let others make mistakes. But above all, empowerment communicates trust and confidence in those who serve on our leadership team. Let your teachers teach, and let your class leaders lead. The effective leader will set the vision, provide the resources, and turn their leaders loose!

(6) *Be passionate and inspire others to work hard.* Effective leaders inspire others to participate and to perform at levels that are above average. Effective leaders have a definite passion for what needs to be done and for those with whom they work. Too often, leaders are content to sit back and just get the work done. Too often, leaders are aloof and not involved with their team members. But the more effective leaders have a contagious passion for the tasks of ministry. If Sunday school and church growth are important, then be passionate about Sunday school and church growth. A passionate leader inspires others to join in and do the extraordinary.

(7) *Stay put and set up shop.* Most ministers change location within two to five years of beginning a ministry. This quick tenure does not build trust or equity with the membership. Some ministers pay half-hearted attention to their jobs while hoping/praying with the other half of their hearts for a better situation. These ministers will always be distracted. They will never be totally emotionally invested with the people they serve. Ministers who are never totally emotionally invested will have a difficult time leading the people to do the ordinary aspects of ministry. They will have an almost impossible time leading others to reach extraordinary heights of ministry. Stay put! Set up shop! Develop a passionate vision! Love the people! Lead them to do extraordinary things! The same is true for Sunday school leadership. Consistent leaders and teachers inspire confidence and trust. As we lead with passion, people respond.

(8) *Major on the main things.* This is the ability of "focus." Leaders who focus are rarely discouraged and disheartened. As we focus, we fire the passion that drives us. Focus on the one event each year that

is your *main* priority. Focus on two to five events that need 50 percent improvement. Focus on 100 things that need 1 percent improvement. Too often, ministers try to reinvent everything in their churches. But everything does not need a complete overhaul. Focus on what really needs your main energies. Give main energy, main resources, and main prayer time to this one priority. Then go to work. Along the way, make partial improvements in the other areas. Every improvement will bring energy to your leadership. As you begin to make "minor" gains in many areas, soon you have made major gains in almost every area. And even better, you have done this with intentional leadership and vision. Intentional leaders instill trust in those with whom they work. Intentional leaders make little changes and inspire confidence.

(9) *Pray, pray, pray!* Nothing great was ever accomplished without a strong base of prayer. Daily prayer keeps us in tune with God. Daily prayer keeps God in tune with us. Spend time daily in prayer for your vision, for your leadership team, for the work to be done, and for your own spirit. Prayer and devotion will develop a strong discipline within you and give you strength for doing the work. Pray without ceasing, stay in tune with God, and let the Spirit guide you.

(10) *Visualize growth and success.* Vision and focus are important. As you visualize what you are going to do, visualize success too. As you visualize growth and success, you will also develop an attitude of embracing change. The reason most of us resist growth is that we are afraid of what we will have to give up. If we visualize growth and success, we will see that what we may have to give up is worth the victory we will gain. People will follow a leader who models positive guidance and successful accomplishment. Grow for it!

Attitude Determines Altitude

A positive attitude is probably the most important aspect of leadership. A positive attitude attracts people to want to join in. A positive attitude energizes those who join with us. A positive attitude encourages others to be positive too. A positive attitude is contagious.

People are often more attracted to positive people rather than to positive ideas. Enthusiastic leaders will bring people into the Sunday school more than negative leaders. An enthusiastic leader models a vibrant faith. As we keep a positive attitude, we communicate that we are strong and mature in our faith. A spirit of optimism will go far in leading us through the tough times and keeping us growing.

The following checklist may help you keep your attitude focused on the positives and keep your growing and maturing as you lead.[2]

Attitude Checklist

Answer Yes or No to each of the statements below:

1. I lead with enthusiasm regardless of the number of persons in my class each week.
2. I lead with creativity regardless of the attitudes of those around me.
3. People and their needs are important to me.
4. Whether I am in charge of the project or not, I participate with a positive attitude.
5. Those who work with me recognize me as a positive leader who models enthusiasm.
6. My class knows that I care about them whether they are in attendance or not.
7. I listen willingly and allow input from all on my leadership team.
8. I patiently listen to criticism without turning negative in response.
9. I rarely blame others for the difficult times that I might endure.
10. I rarely blame my mistakes on the leadership team with which I work.
11. I have a similar attitude for life, whether at church, at play, or at work.
12. When other leaders/teachers are criticized, I rarely join in the critical conversations.
13. I look forward to every leadership event for what I can share about the experience.
14. I look forward to every leadership event for what I can learn from others.
15. I try to discipline myself to be positive in the goodness, grace, and love of Christ.

The "yes" responses indicate a positive attitude toward Sunday school leadership. The "no" responses indicate areas that need reorientation toward the positive.

Effective Leaders Plan for Success

Effective teachers/leaders must have a good plan for success. Planning is crucial for the class, for the Sunday school, and for the Sunday school leadership team. Planning keeps us focused on a balance of tasks and people. As we plan well, we make sure to take care of the details and to meet the ministry needs. Good planning leads to good teaching and attentive administration. Good planning ensures focused attention on all that we do in the leading and teaching functions of Sunday school work.

- *Planning improves communication and coordination.* As you plan by yourself and with your leadership team, you are forced to communicate. As you broaden your planning to include the Sunday school leadership team, you get a sense of what coordination efforts are required.
- *Planning enhances achieving goals.* As you plan, you are able to see what's missing. As you set goals, planning helps you develop a framework for meeting those goals. Planning lets you get ready, helps you work intentionally, helps you achieve!
- *Planning focuses on the "big picture" as well as the "small stuff."* Planning must come from a big idea that drives you with enthusiasm. Planning must also include the details by which you will work to achieve the big idea. As you plan, you develop the direction and the goal. Successful planning also anticipates the details that need to be taken care of successfully.
- *Planning makes provision for ongoing training opportunities.* Along the way, you will need to keep your leadership team focused. Effective planning helps you introduce training opportunities. Training will keep your workers learning, enthusiastic, and united in pursuing the goals.

• *Planning builds a strong team spirit.* As you plan to succeed, enthusiasm grows. Planning together provides for input from your team. Planning keeps everyone focused, encouraging one another, recovering from mistakes, and growing together.
• *Planning gives objective benchmarks for evaluation.* As you set realistic goals, you then know what you want to achieve. As these goals are in place, you then evaluate based on your progress toward the goals. Planning helps keep you on task from the beginning and gives you points for evaluation along the way.

So What?

Planning, focused, and enthusiastic leaders make a positive difference in the lives of those who come to Sunday school. Sunday school growth only happens in the context of effective leadership and effective teaching. Growth never happens accidentally. Growth happens within the context of intentional leadership.

The Sunday school leadership team, the Sunday school teaching faculty, and the Sunday school class leaders are all important leaders in the Sunday school. These leaders are all a part of helping the Sunday school to grow.

Effective and efficient leaders will impact your church for continued and contagious Sunday school growth! Effective leadership makes visitors feel welcome. Effective leadership undergirds the work of teachers and class leaders. Effective leadership plans, directs, evaluates, and redirects the entire, ongoing work of the Sunday school. Effective leadership communicates that your Sunday school is prepared for and cares for the people who are participating Sunday after Sunday.

The two basic questions facing leaders today demand answers. Answering these in a positive way is crucial for effective leadership to grow and develop.

• *How much do I exercise power and authority?*
• *How much freedom do I allow other leaders?*

As we begin to answer these questions, we begin to solve the leadership puzzle. As we begin to solve the leadership puzzle, we begin to grow and develop as more positive and effective leaders. The growth of your congregation is too important to ignore the answers to these questions!

Trust God, pray daily, and lead on bravely!

Notes

[1]Robert Greenleaf, *The Servant as Leader* (San Francisco: Jossey-Bass Publishers, 1996), 1-16.

[2] D. Bruce and R. Bruce, *Growing a Great Sunday School Class* (Nashville: Abingdon, 1994), 15-22.

Chapter Five

Building Block 4—Relevant Teaching

Teaching people isn't what it used to be! In the good old days people came to Sunday school for information, inspiration, and fellowship. They sat still while we instilled in them what we had distilled through study. Teaching was simpler, less complicated, and pressure free. They come to us today for similar reasons; however, their expectations are higher. People leave their high-technology homes filled with high-technology inventions. They arrive at church in their high-technology cars. They come in designer clothes, from designer homes, looking for challenge, inspiration, and interaction.

We usher them into our less than state-of-the-art classrooms. Most Sunday school rooms have the same pine-paneled walls and carpet that were there fifty years ago. None of us would have carpet in our homes for fifty years! We pay little or no attention to the physical environment that affects our learning. We pay even less attention to the emotional and intellectual environment of Sunday school. We just tell them what they need to know with little emotion. We tend to dump guilt on our classes and send them off to worship. For many churches, teaching is still a "you sit still and I'll instill" approach. However, effective teaching is far more than just "telling and yelling." (Yes, this is a bit of a cartoon, but, sadly, this is still very close to some realities!)

The ability to teach people biblical truths is one of the most challenging aspects of ministry in our churches today. Teaching is crucial to helping others grow and mature as followers of Christ. As teachers, we present challenges, information, and inspiration week after week. We have immediate access to the resources that enhance our teaching. The Internet, interactive commentaries, and other Bible resource support are readily available for teaching preparation. But learners also have immediate access to these resources. In many cases, learners are coming to class better prepared and more informed than many teachers are! Good teachers know that they can no longer bluff their way through a lesson.

Effective and challenging teaching is a critical building block of the Sunday school. Therefore, why do so many teachers prepare the night before? Why do so many teachers approach this assignment with indifference? Why do so many teachers use poor teaching methods? Why do so many teachers refuse to contact class members and prospects? Why do so many teachers basically ignore the duties assigned them?

Possibly many teachers don't really understand what is required of them as teachers. Perhaps some teachers are pushed in their weekly schedules and have less and less time for preparation. Probably, most of our teachers are serving out of a real desire to be effective but need teaching ideas to keep them fresh. All of those who teach need consistent training, resources, and helps.

Our challenge is to equip teachers with effective teaching methods and resources. One task is to help our teachers be as prepared as possible each week. Another task is to model for them effective outreach and ministry methods to be able to care for learners. Yet another task is to give the teachers tools to organize and grow their classes.

By blending traditional teaching methods with innovative approaches, Sunday school can be fun, inspirational, and relational. By blending tradition with innovation, Sunday school can grow, both numerically and spiritually. As we blend traditional methods of Sunday school ministry with innovative and creative approaches for the twenty-first century, we open ourselves up to be used more effectively by our Heavenly Father. As we make ourselves more open to God, we position ourselves to build community and, maybe, impact our world!

People Go Where They Know

"People go where they know they are prepared for and cared for." This statement continues to be a guide and motivator for every aspect of my ministry. The statement is guiding me even as I write this chapter!

As a teacher (regardless of the age group we teach), one task is to communicate to those who come each week that we are prepared for them. When we guide the class session with confidence, when we are open to class discussions, and when we are able to give leadership to the class session, we communicate our preparation. When we have support materials ready, when handouts are prepared, when the chairs are arranged, we communicate our preparation. When we know exactly what the goals of our class session are, we communicate our preparation. As we communicate good preparation, we also communicate that we care.

As a teacher, we are also to care for our class! We are in the people business. The needs of the institution must never come before the needs of the people. As we prepare for them, we communicate that we care. As we contact them when they're absent and challenge them when they're present, we communicate that we care. As we cry with them when they hurt and celebrate with them in important times, we communicate that we care. People go where they know they have been prepared for and are cared for.

"Prepared for and cared for" doesn't happen automatically. We have to be intentional in our preparation and our caring. Being intentional means that we schedule and protect times for preparing each day. Being intentional means that we schedule and honor time each week for calling class members and prospects simply to check in and say hello.

Effective teachers prepare so that they can help others to learn. Effective teachers prepare so that they can help others to grow spiritually. Effective teachers prepare in order to be enthusiastic, warm, and sensitive as they lead the class session each week. The attitude that the teacher brings to the class session each week greatly affects the learning climate and the growth potential of the class. "Prepared for and cared for" helps keep the teacher focused on being intentional in the teaching role.

As we teach intentionally, there are several outcomes that we can anticipate:

• *Growth in Belief.* As God's Word challenges us, we grow deeper in our spirituality. Consistently encountering biblical truth leads us to closeness with God and with one another. As we grow in our beliefs, we are better prepared to be servants in the kingdom of God. Intentional teaching helps us lead others to deeper spiritual maturity.

• *Growth in Community.* As God's Word challenges us, we grow deeper in our intimacy with one another. There is no way to sit in a Sunday school class week after week and not grow friendships. Growing friendships in our class helps us then reach out to others, both inside the church and outside the church. Intentional teaching fosters relationships that add meaning to the body life of the church family.

• *Growth in Servanthood.* As God's Word challenges us, we grow deeper in our service to one another. We are not to teach to entertain; we are called to equip. As we teach with purpose and intentionality, we challenge those in our classes to grow in their own service. We are all called to be servants of Christ. As we grow in our servanthood, we enrich the church.

• *Growth in Attendance.* If we are growing in belief, community, and servanthood, the message of our "great" class is going to spread. Most people want to be around good things that are happening. Your class members will tell others in the church about the class. Your class members will tell others not in the church about the class. You will begin reaching out more and reaching in more. Intentional preparation leads to effective teaching. Effective teaching leads to growth!

Do preschoolers need to grow in belief and community and servanthood? What about children? Do youth and adults need to grow in these areas? Do we need to reach others for our church? Do we need to reach out to our community? The answer to each of these is "Absolutely!"

Intentional teaching leads us to prepare daily and to care consistently for those who come to us each week. As we do so, we will grow significantly, both numerically and spiritually. "Prepared for and cared for" leads others to prepare and care as well.

The following tips will help you as you begin to be more intentional about communicating "prepared for and cared for" to those who come to your class:

• *Acceptance.* Accept the learner where he/she is. You will have some learners who have been in church all their lives. You will have others who have just begun to attend. You will have to be flexible in helping all to grow and participate. Don't worry, you cannot "mess up" anyone's spiritual growth. God is guiding the process! Your task is to love and care for each one who comes into your classroom. Your task is to guide them as they search for meaning from Scripture. They will grow in God's love. Teach them, love them, and help them grow. Leave the results to God.

• *Growth and Development.* Be aware of the developmental stages your class members are experiencing. Know the general theories on growth and development for the age group you teach. All ages are in some stage of growth and development, even adults. Pay attention to these stages and be flexible as learners grow and develop.

Ask parents to keep you aware of changes their preschoolers, children, and youth may be experiencing. A preschooler in the midst of "potty training" will definitely challenge your flexibility. Likewise, a child exerting independence, a youth experiencing puberty, and an adult dealing with an empty nest will also challenge your flexibility and teaching approaches. Know your learners, accept them as individuals, and be flexible.

• *Motivation.* Try to understand the "why" and "what" of your learners. Why do they attend Sunday school? What do they really want to learn? Pay attention to the friendships they have and make, pay attention to the parents' expectations, and be sensitive to the needs of each person in the class. As you understand better why they are coming and what they want from the class, you will be in a better position to teach creatively and with more freedom. This creativity and freedom will help you grow into a better teacher. These aspects will definitely make your students more at ease in the growth environment.

• *Involvement.* Yes, the learners need to be involved in the learning process. As teachers, however, we also need to be involved with our learners beyond the Sunday morning experience. As you attend sporting events, band concerts, debates, gymnastics, and recitals, you learn more about your learners and their homes. As you visit in their homes, you learn even more. The more you learn about your class members, the more effective you will be as a teacher.

Be sensitive to the spiritual condition of your learners. You will have some who have been Christians a long time. You will have some learners who are new Christians or who are searching right now to know Christ. Be sensitive to the spiritual growth and development of each learner and how you can help them grow in Christ. Effective teaching is as much about relationships as it is about content and methodology.

• *Affirmation.* Take time to affirm learners. Affirmation goes a long way in motivating learners to continue their faith journeys. Frequent affirmation will keep your learners feeling prepared for and cared for.

Send birthday cards, "we missed you" cards, and celebration cards. Make periodic phone calls just to check in with your class members. Take time to thank them when they do special things. Sincere affirmation, not empty praise, will go a long way in building loyalty and growing a wonderful Sunday school class.

Today's learners are sophisticated, busy, and overwhelmed in many areas of their lives. Intentional teachers help build friendships among class members, bridge biblical truths into everyday applications, and balance the many demands of life with Christian servanthood. And, as we grow in these areas, we will also find ourselves reaching more people that we ever thought possible.

Teaching Is More Than Telling

Can you imagine a preschool class in which all the students sit quietly while the teacher lectures for an hour? How absurd and ridiculous is that? We know that preschoolers are active learners. They learn best in an environment that stimulates their senses and encourages them to explore. The lecture method does not work well in this environment.

Actually, the lecture method is not the most effective teaching method with any age group. The most effective teaching method is the method that *involves* the learners in the teaching/learning process. The least effective teaching method is the one you use all the time! Teach with creativity and variety. Teach to help learners discover truths for themselves. One of my favorite prayer sentences is "Help me remember, Lord, that all the truth I know is *not* all the truth!" Effective teachers build upon the experiences of all their learners. As we share with each other in the class, we learn and grow together.

Jesus modeled this approach for us. He used a variety of teaching methods—sometimes stories, sometimes humor, sometimes question and answer, sometimes lecture. His preparation and care for those around Him guided the teaching experience. He built upon the experiences of the learners around Him. As a wise and prepared teacher, He was sensitive to the teachable moment and flexible enough to balance a variety of teaching methods. Jesus was a creative, inspiring, and motivating instructor. He was molding a community of learners into friends. He was preparing His followers to become servants of God.

If you teach preschoolers and children, plan on using five to eight different teaching approaches during a class session. Activity-oriented learning is highly recommended for these ages. Choose activities that include music, art, and sensory stimulation. Tell stories, sing, paint, run, play with toys, eat fun foods. Crawl around on the floor with them. Play games with them. Let your "inner child" come out and play. Help the children enjoy the hour and grow in their spiritual selves.

If you teach youth and adults, plan on using three to five different teaching approaches during a class session. Discussion, questions and answers, research, creative writing, even a dash of drama will keep the learning environment lively. Don't get too "cute" with the exercises, but let Bible learning be fun, interactive, and thought-provoking. Allow older youth and adults plenty of time to interact and share their thoughts while also hearing the thoughts of the teacher. (Of course, fun foods are always a plus here too!) Guide the learning experience to include all who attend the class. Teach learners and help them to think. Help them to think critically, to examine the Bible and decide for themselves what God is saying to His people.

Don't make the mistake of trying to tell the class participants everything they need to know. Guide them to make exciting discoveries on their own. This applies to all age groups. Discovery learning is fun, motivational, and exciting. Activity-oriented learning also has higher retention rates, especially for youth and adult learners.

Find creative and interactive ways to present materials. Find ways to teach lesson materials so that learners can discuss some information together. Teaching, when it is done best, is relational and fosters sharing.

While many frown on the lecture method, there are appropriate times for this method. When you do lecture (to adults and youth), do so in short blocks. Never lecture for more than ten minutes without a break.

Plan your teaching session in blocks using a variety of teaching methods. Decide what are the two or three most important truths or challenges that you wish to convey. Let these be the pillars around which you build your lecture. Then supplement your lecture with question and answer or sharing times to bring impact to the teaching.

The following guidelines will help you build toward meaningful teaching and learning in the classroom:

• *Give learners ample opportunities to participate in the learning experience.* Passive learning does little or nothing to grow learners. Active learning lets everyone present participate and learn from one another. Learners enjoy talking with one another and learning from one another. Learners learn best when they are involved in the teaching/learning process.

• *Give learners opportunities to apply lesson truths to their lives.* Learners today are conditioned to instant feedback. We are in a world of fast-paced lifestyles. To keep learner motivation high, provide immediate feedback and affirmation. This will keep the class experiences relevant and discussion focused on vital life issues. Relevant and practical experiences, for all age groups, will make a difference in their interest and consistent attendance.

• *Give learners opportunities periodically to understand the big picture of Scripture.* Too often we emphasize short little segments of Scripture. We spotlight Bible stories or Bible truths but fail to show how these fit in the bigger story of redemption. We even encourage memorization of Bible verses with little or no application. From time to time, remind learners how these "little pieces" relate to the total picture of God's redemptive love. Jesus summed up the whole of God's work in two commandments, "Love God with all your heart, soul and mind, with all of your being, and love your neighbor as much as you love yourself" (my paraphrase). We need to remind learners occasionally how the little parts fit together.

• *Give learners your priority attention in the classroom.* Be "learner-oriented" and "teacher-flexible." The teaching/learning process begins when the first person arrives. The teacher should always arrive before class participants! Teach with the learner in mind. Teach to keep the learning environment open, involving, and exciting. Be flexible.

Practice "baby philosophy"—if something "stinks," change it! If what you've planned to do is not working, simply change your approach. As you plan, have several ideas in mind that you can substitute for an approach that is not working. Always have several teaching methods ready to go. Don't let your ego get in the way of sharing the exciting truths of God's Word.

• *Give learners opportunities for honest sharing.* Good Bible teaching provides a climate of honesty and safety. Innovative Sunday school classes allow for times of laughter and for tears. Exciting Bible teaching allows for fun and for serious interaction. Use positive examples of humor, use honest life illustrations, and be open to the leadership of God's spirit in the growth, maturity, and intimacy of your class.

An ineffective teacher can ruin an exciting learning experience. An ego-driven teacher can squelch interaction and relational learning. A controlling teacher can stifle relationship building and spiritual growth. Let your preparation grow your confidence. Trust your prayer life to guide you toward the truths that will directly impact your class. Don't be afraid to say to your class "I don't know...but I will find out!" Openness and honesty will go far in building a loving and accepting Sunday school class.

Be creative as a teacher. Be prepared and caring. Be flexible. These words will go far to help you grow as a teacher, regardless of the age group you teach. Preschoolers, children, youth, and adults all want to be challenged with the excitement of biblical truths. Above all, be confident in the power of Christ. Enter every teaching opportunity filled with confidence that you have done your best each week to open yourself up to the loving power of God. Teach with confidence and sensitivity. Leave the results to God, and be assured that blessings and miracles are going to abound.

Snap, Crackle, Pop, Zip!

Teaching with a variety of teaching methods adds spice to our classrooms. When we "spice things up," the learning environment will sizzle! Remember, we don't have to overload the senses of our classes every week. If you teach preschoolers and children, use five to eight different teaching approaches. If you teach youth or adults, use three to five different teaching approaches. Know the needs of your class and the pace at which they like to learn. Grow for it!

The following teaching approaches are areas where we can add sizzle to our teaching:

• *Paper/pencil/print.* All learners can respond to these exercises. You may have to use crayons instead of pencils with younger ages, but printed materials do teach. All ages respond well to the printed page. Lists of true/false responses, fill in the blank questions, word search puzzles, and many more printed activities help to enhance learning. All ages beyond the preschool years respond well to reading and writing. Invite learners to read aloud from the Bible. Invite learners to share inspirational poems. Share texts from other readings to amplify the lesson. Use these materials to motivate your learners to deeper levels of interaction.

• *Visuals.* These materials include videos, computers, charts, maps, posters—more than just a printed page or a crayon activity. Show short clips of a video (three to five minutes in length. Don't use video as a "baby-sitting" tool or simply to take up time!) Use charts, maps, and posters to elaborate your teaching points with youth and adults. Expand learner attention with a demonstration or brief dramatic presentation. Preschoolers and younger children love visual stimulation. Find creative ways to spice up your teaching with a variety of visuals.

• *Audio.* Audio tapes, computer-generated sounds, dramatic readings, and lectures expand the teaching tools at our disposal. Introduce a new unit of study with a Bible character sharing some insights. Play an audio tape clip (again no longer than five minutes) to add to the teaching. Enlist class members prior to class to assist in a dramatic reading or vocal choir. Again, remember, when you lecture, do so in short bits of 8–10 minutes at a time. Then supplement your lectures with other teaching methods.

• *Touch or Tactile.* All age groups love hands-on activities. Drawing and coloring, pencil and paper activities, model building, and manipulating objects are ways to expand your teaching. You may have some biblical artifacts that you can share. You may have other objects that can help excite learners. Preschoolers and children love to pet animals. Look around and see how you can bring the Bible to life. Let your learners "touch" the Bible and excite their learning.

• *Personal Interaction.* Small group experiences, discussion/question and answer sessions, debate, and sharing times allow for more creative approaches to Bible teaching. Youth and adults are especially motivated when sharing their thoughts and opinions with others. Older preschoolers and children also enjoy small group work. Most every session outline in Sunday school literature allows for small group and personal interactions.

• *Activity Learning.* Active learning is that which uses our psychomotor skills. Standing up and moving around, clapping our hands, drawing, acting, games, and more help break up the monotony of sitting and listening for a lesson. As we get the blood flowing to the brain, we stimulate the learner. Get 'em up and moving around; get 'em up and active! As you do, learning is strengthened and remembered.

• *Taste and Smell.* This approach brings the learner into the world of the Bible. Eating and drinking foods of the Bible are a great approach. When you talk about salt and light, remind learners of salt (or of no salt!). Foods from Bible lands are readily available today. Bring these to class, share these with learners, and let them experience firsthand instead of just telling learners about the foods.

• *Music.* I know, I know . . . this could be in the "audio" section. But music is just an area all its own. We don't use music enough in our class experiences. Scripture invites us to "make a joyful noise" as praise to God. Preschoolers and children love singing and use music frequently. Somehow, as we get older, we forget the joy (and the learning) that can come from singing. Find ways to spice up your teaching with music. Excite the learner, inspire the learner, *sing*!

Since many learners have no idea about their learning preferences, our job as teacher is to share a variety of teaching methods. As we add "spice" to the learning environment, we get an idea of what our learners appreciate and how they learn. A teacher sensitive to the needs and reactions of his/her class will vary teaching methods to excite all the learners in the class.

One tip: when using a variety of learning activities with youth and adults, give the time that you are allowing for the experience. For instance, "For the next three minutes we're going to listen to an audio tape of . . . . " Or "For the next five minutes, I want you to work in small groups to . . . . " The reason for this disclaimer is to help all learners relax. Some learners may not enjoy this learning approach, but all of us can endure a three to five minute learning experience. An interactive person will understand that you are not going to lecture for an hour. A shy person will understand that the small group experience will not last forever. A thinking person will hear that we aren't going to play games for the entire class session. Remember, people go where they know they've been prepared for and are cared for. As we give them time limits for the variety of teaching methods, we are again letting learners know that we have prepared for them and that we care for them.

So, how can you learn these creative approaches? There are a number of "methods" resource books available for teachers. There are many creative teachers in your congregation. Consult some of these specialized books and talk to some of these teachers. Then, apply what you discover to your Sunday school class setting.

The following are general guidelines for creative teaching for each age group. They are by no means exhaustive. These guidelines simply provide a general overview of each of the age groups. You will want to consult other, more specialized resources for help in greater detail.

Preschoolers

• *Modeling.* Preschoolers learn through imitating what they see around them. When preschoolers see and hear others around them doing things, they jump in too. The preschool teacher learns to model and encourage the preschoolers to "help," "share," and "follow." Preschoolers are good imitators.

• *Discovery.* Preschoolers learn through exploring their curiosity. As preschoolers begin to explore the world around them, their curiosity kicks in and they learn. This discovery process is part of the joy of the learning journey. Preschoolers are highly curious.

• *Activity.* Preschoolers learn by actively doing and playing. Preschoolers learn independence by doing. Repetition is a good approach to use with preschoolers. Preschoolers learn to explore and imitate sometimes through playing. We allow our preschoolers to touch, taste, smell, see, hear, and do. As they participate actively through task and play, preschoolers learn to share with others around them. Preschoolers are active learners.

• *Affirmation.* Preschoolers learn by continued encouragement and support. There is nothing more sad than hurting a preschooler's spirit. Preschoolers bring such energy and excitement to the learning environment. We affirm their learning and continue encouraging them as we guide them. There is nothing more moving than a preschooler with a huge self-satisfied grin on his/her face.

• *Relationships.* Preschoolers learn through their interaction with their teachers and with each other. As they share, they learn feelings, attitudes, and concepts. Preschoolers learn much as they relate to one another in social settings. What a joy to watch preschoolers share hugs on Sunday morning.

Children

• *Discovery.* Children are curious by nature. This curiosity helps guide their learning and discovery. Children are curious about God. Children are curious about one another. This curiosity leads them to discover great truths about their world. Our joy is guiding them to discover and watching the delight in their eyes as they do.

• *Activity.* Children learn by active involvement. Children learn and grow by doing, playing, writing, coloring, building. Children learn to explore and imitate through all these activities. We teach them by guiding an exploration through all of their senses. As they participate actively through task and play, children learn truths about life, truths about themselves, and spiritual truth too. Children learn about God as they interact with one another. What a special moment for a teacher of children to see those children come to a living faith in Christ!

• *Affirmation.* Children learn by continued encouragement and support. There is nothing more sad than damaging a child's spirit to learn. Children bring such energy to the classroom. While we try to direct their energy and excitement to the learning tasks, we must do so without heavy authority, guilt, or control. We affirm their learning abilities and encourage them as we guide them. There is nothing more moving than watching a child who has accomplished something special.

• *Relationships.* Friendships are a critical part of a child's learning. Friendships with their peers and their teachers are important to learning at this age. During the building of friendships, children also learn about themselves and their world. Children learn about God as they learn about one another. How joyful to see children holding hands, skipping down the hall at church, singing "Jesus Loves Me"!

• *Stimulation and Motivation.* As children grow and develop, they begin to seek out stimulating and motivating learning activities. Effective teachers pay attention to this growth and development and continue finding ways to challenge, motivate, and guide. Effective teachers continue helping children grow and develop even as they prepare for adolescence. Children are not only the future of our church, they are also important to the community *right now*!

Youth

• *Activity.* Youth learn by doing. They love to let their imaginations run wild. They are stimulated by doing and then discussing. Youth enjoy being involved in planning, doing, and evaluating the learning processes. Activity-oriented learning with youth allows for a depth of discussion and interaction. Activity-oriented learning allows for a depth of spiritual searching and growth. What a great experience to see a young person have an "aha!" moment in their spiritual growth.

• *Relationships.* Youth are relationship-driven. If their friends come to Sunday school, they will come. If their friends participate and interact, they will do so as well. Friendships are crucial to the learning of youth. Friendships with their peers and their teachers are important. Youth need to know that they can come to a safe place and be in a safe environment. Youth need to know that the friendships they make will serve them well in their learning and their growth. As youth grow and learn from friends, they also learn about themselves, their God, and God's Word. There is a joy in seeing a young, timid sixth grader grow in wisdom and stature and develop into a mature, responsible young adult!

• *Emotions.* Youth are riding an emotional roller coaster. As we teach them, there will be times when they react with great emotion and do not understand why. As we guide them to deal honestly with their emotions, we help them learn how to express themselves appropriately. The young Jesus also had to learn to express His emotions appropriately. Use sensitivity and compassion and help youth grow in an emotional and spiritual maturity that will serve them well into adulthood. Youth are the church of the future; they are also the church of today.

• *Concrete and Abstract.* Youth are at the age and stage to think both in a concrete way and an abstract way. Youth can concretely express their faith. Youth can conceptualize models for faith expression also. Don't be frustrated as a teacher, and don't frustrate youth learners by locking in on one way of teaching. Youth love variety. They love activity. Find ways to present lesson truths in a variety of teaching methods. Allow youth to express themselves in concrete and abstract ways. The youth of today are some of the most gifted and talented people in history. Give these talented persons freedom to explore, to grow, and to develop into wonderfully gifted Christians. We need the salt and light that they bring to our world.

Adults

• *Activity.* Adults can learn and do learn every day. We too often make Sunday school for adults so boring that adult learners shut down. While lecture is one good approach to teaching adults, there are many more effective approaches to teaching. Adults need sensory stimulation just as the other age groups do. Adults desire interaction, active learning, a comfortable environment, and a variety of teaching methods. Involve the adults in the sharing of the learning experience. Adult learning is exciting!

• *Relationships.* Adults enjoy learning from one another. Adults are inspired and motivated by interaction with other adult learners. Not everyone wishes to share the depth of their feelings, but all adults enjoy talking and participating in fellowship and learning activities. As adults build relationships in their classes, they will also reach out to their friends and family members and bring them to church too. Now that is exciting!

• *Multisensory.* Adults learn best when all their senses are involved in the learning experience. Use a variety of teaching methods to keep all learners involved in the learning experience. Stimulate adults by touching all of their senses. As you do, the Bible will come alive, perhaps for the very first time. When adults get excited about learning, many of them also get excited about teaching.

• *Application.* Adult learners are looking for life application! By now you know that adult learners need excitement, interaction, and a meaning to the message. As adults see and feel how the biblical message applies to their lives, they will participate and grow. Be intellectual in your teaching; adult learners take learning very seriously. Be serious in your presentation; frivolity will turn off adult learners. Be fun in your teaching; adult learners do want to enjoy the process. But, above all, have practical application for their lives. As you guide adults to meaning and truth, they will grow to become leaders in your church and God's kingdom.

So What?

For all of these age groups, you have to begin the teaching journey by teaching! Trial and error is a wonderful teacher. If your class knows that you are prepared for them and care about them, they will give you grace as you discover your confidence.

The best way to learn what works is to try something new. Yes, you might be uncomfortable at first. Yes, the class might give you a little grief, but they will participate if you lead with confidence. Practice, practice, practice! Involve your learners, have fun, and let the learning soar. With a little practice and lots of preparation, you will become a most exciting and interactive teacher. The depth of your learning experiences will amaze you. You may even witness a miracle happening through those wonderful chunky Crayolas!

Trust God, prepare thoroughly, and teach bravely!

Chapter Six

Building Block 5—Outreach & Inreach

You never get a second chance to make a first impression. People come to us from all over the community and we have to respond to them. Their first visit with us sets their expectation levels for ministry (if they ever come again). Their subsequent visits determine whether they join us in ministry and fellowship.

The ways we reach out to prospects determine whether or not they choose to join our church. The ways we reach in to those enrolled in our classes (but not yet church members) determine continued numerical and spiritual growth. Outreach is ministry oriented to visitors, church guests, and church prospects. Inreach is ministry oriented to church members, Sunday school members, and "regular" visitors or prospective members of your church.

People generally visit church the first time because they've heard something intriguing or exciting about the ministry of the church. People generally return because something has peaked their interest. We need to provide multiple entry points for those visitors to make their way into the fellowship of our church. We need to take care to be culturally relevant, user-friendly, and authentic as we present these opportunities. The following ideas represent some of the reasons why visitors return to our church.

Six Reasons Why Visitors Return

(1) A Positive Congregational Self-Esteem. When visitors come to the church and feel uplifted by the members they encounter, they will usually return. When members feel that their church is a special place and has something to offer, visitors sense this positive energy. We communicate a positive congregational self-esteem when visitors are spoken to cordially and when people go out of their way to make visitors welcome. We communicate a positive congregational self-esteem when we contact visitors within twenty-four hours of their *first* visit. We communicate a positive congregational self-esteem when we smile and greet one another in the hallways and gathering spaces of the church facility.

We also communicate a positive congregational self-esteem when our facilities, printed materials, and church direction signs communicate quality. When paint flakes off the walls, when dirt and dust collect in the corners of the rooms, when rest room facilities are dirty and not furnished, we communicate poor self-esteem. When church bulletins are poorly printed with multiple grammatical errors and spelling mistakes, we communicate poor self-esteem. When the direction signs are poorly designed or non-existent, we communicate poor self-esteem. The way we take care of our facilities and present our church to those who visit speaks volumes about how we feel about our church.

(2) Congregational Unity. When visitors enter the church building, they get a feel for the unity of our congregation. Visitors listen to hear how we share greetings with one another. Visitors watch to see how we hug, shake hands, or respond to each other. Visitors try to get a feel for the "love and harmony" within our church. They get a sense of how unified we are based on how they see and hear us interacting. Very few people want to be part of a congregation filled with anger, conflict, and strife. If major conflicts are at play in a congregation, the stress will be obvious. When anger and stress are evident, people will be distant and disconnected. Who wants to be a part of a church like that?

People look for a church that is relevant to their life needs. They look for a church that will help them deal with their stress. Few people want to join a church so that they can join in the stress and anger of a local congregation! People come to a congregation looking for a spirit of vitality, of unity, and of harmony. They can tell if we are not all moving in a similar direction, working with a common vision.

(3) Enthusiasm of Pastor and Staff Ministers. Most of us are drawn to and motivated by enthusiastic leadership. Enthusiasm is infectious! Enthusiastic preaching, music, and teaching excite visitors. Enthusiastic sermons motivate the rest of us to be involved and more committed. When pastors preach with excitement and confidence, they inspire hope in the congregation. Dynamic worship motivates all of us, especially those who visit. When staff ministers lead worship and teach classes with energy and a positive presence, they fill the congregation with enthusiasm for growth. When pastor and staff ministers are excited about growth and change, the congregation catches the vision and joins in the excitement.

Visitors look for an attitude of growth and confidence from ministers. People looking for a church home want a place of positive energy and forward thinking. When we communicate our energy with a sincere spirit, careful not to turn people away with overly positive thinking or exaggerated posturing, we lead others to want to share in what we have. Energy and enthusiasm draw people to our congregations.

(4) Vital Ministries. A church preaching and teaching inside its walls must be active in vital ministries to the world. Growing churches have a variety of ministries that continue to add relevance to their community. A church with a positive congregational self-esteem strives to make a difference in their community and beyond. When a church provides ministry to the community, they authenticate the message they preach week in and week out. When a church is involved in the community, they communicate a strong belief in the message of Christ's love. This involvement communicates faith, hope, and love to their community.

Visitors want to be a part of a meaningful program. Those who come back to the church want to know that they are not just going to "sit and soak." Visitors want to be a part of vital ministries both inside and outside the church walls. Community service from a Christian perspective stretches us all. Christian community service sometimes puts us in places where we normally wouldn't travel. Christian community service transforms us from people simply hearing a message to people living a message. Visitors are attracted to this kind of energy and relevant faith. Visitors are attracted to a church that puts into practice what it preaches.

(5) Opportunities for Small-Group Study and Fellowship. We must provide multiple entry points for visitors coming to our congregations. These entry points are more than just the outside doors. Small-group opportunities allow for relationships to be formed. Small-group opportunities allow for discussion of relevant faith issues. The first important entry point for today's church is the worship service. However, while worship may be exciting and uplifting, this is hardly a small-group setting. Visitors attending worship can be anonymous and slip in and out of the building. When they attend a small group, however, they begin to get a better feel for the intimacy of the fellowship.

Sunday school classes, small-group Bible studies, missions groups, work groups, athletic teams, book studies, women's groups, men's groups—there are a myriad of small-group opportunities for entry points. Many churches offer weekday childcare, weekly music lessons, support and recovery groups, even financial management and executive coaching opportunities.

One key is for the small group to be contemporary, culturally and spiritually relevant, and user-friendly. Look around your community and become sensitive to the spiritual needs. Train your Sunday school classes and other small groups to look for and respond to the needs. Teach adults in Sunday school and small-group studies about the importance of being active in the community. Visitors will respond with enthusiasm as they see your church reaching out to the community.

(5) A "Constant Contact" Attitude. One other key is to develop a "constant contact" approach. When visitors attend the church, we need to make every effort to contact them within twenty-four hours of their visit. We must make sure we contact them within the first week. If we fail to make contact, we've lost an opportunity for a positive first impression. When prospects and church members are absent, contacting them within the week of their absence is crucial. Our constant contacting can be in the form of notes, greeting cards, phone calls, e-mail, or any combination of these. The important thing is that we communicate our care for their absence. Under *no circumstances* should we manipulate them with guilt or shame for their absence! We are to contact them because of sincere love and concern.

(6) Sincere & Authentic Relationships. Too many churches today are characterized by slick marketing campaigns, spiritual spin, and "too perfect" projections of themselves. This approach may draw visitors once, but the key to reaching people is through sincere and authentic relationships with them. Visitors are looking to see if we really do believe what we say we believe. Visitors are testing us to see if we are honest about our mission/vision. A slick approach may look good on the front end, but sooner or later, this resembles little more than a "sleazy" attempt to manipulate people.

Christianity is based on sincerity and honesty. We have to be authentic about our faith and how it influences our daily living. We must make every effort to be ministry-based, people-centered, and sincere in our approaches to our community.

As we provide these opportunities, visitors respond positively and begin to assimilate easier. Small groups allow for people to make friends quicker, to get a clearer picture of the church, and to begin to find places for service. These groups represent a variety of interests and activities to which people can more readily explore and join the ministries and fellowship of the congregation.

Positive Outreach Efforts

The impression that we leave with those who visit makes a big difference. Do you have a guest registration center? Do you have greeters in the parking lot? Do you have name tags for members and guests? How easily can guests find their way around your building? How easily can guests assimilate into an existing class or small group? The answers to these questions will have a big impact on your effectiveness in reaching out to the community.

Of course, the most effective outreach effort is a personal touch. Everywhere you go, you have the opportunity to make an impression on prospects for your church. When you attend community and recreational events, or meet with business contacts, you are a witness for Christ and for your church. When you go to the grocery store, the drug store, the convenient store, or the fast food place, you leave an impression to prospective persons for your church. Find the best approach for your personality and share your faith and your church.

How can we do that without being a fanatic or an aggressive (even obnoxious) Christian? Build relationships "FIRST"! Building relationships FIRST is an acrostic that helps us think about ways to make conversation and share ourselves in relaxed approaches. No, we don't share all this every time, but these are just some ideas for keeping a conversation going.

Relationships FIRST to Build Rapport

F We engage others to talk about *Family Status*. We share whether we are married or single, if we have children at home, where we live. What does your family enjoy about church? What does your family enjoy about Sunday school? Talking about family and learning about the prospect's family will help build rapport.

I We share our *Identity*. The "I" reminds us to share where we are from, the area where we grew up, and what we like about the area. This also allows us to talk about our work and what we do there. Everyone I know does some kind of work. You might also share about the work you do at church. You may want to share what your "identity" is within the church—how you see yourself. The identity part of the conversation allows us to find common ground around our identity.

R We build *Rapport.* As we build rapport, we talk about some of the "special" parts of our personality. We might mention our hobbies, our favorite foods or eating places, our favorite movies or television shows, sports, books, music, etc. Think about what interests you at church and what intrigues you about faith. Share areas where common interests with others have helped you grow. Find some areas of common ground and build a friendship upon these.

S We enjoy *Special Events.* As you share with your friend, tell them some of the special aspects of your church that you appreciate. For instance, your Sunday school class would certainly be something to share. You could also tell about some special programs, divorce recovery, marriage enrichment, choir programs, mission opportunities, and other events. If a special event is coming up, *invite* them to the event with enthusiasm. Enjoying special events together adds excitement to your friendship.

T We work to build *Trust.* In building rapport, you don't want to be too aggressive. Instead of overwhelming acquaintances with information and evangelism, take time to build trust. Share some of the basics of your church and possibly your faith, but do so with sincerity.

"T" could also be *Time.* We use our time carefully. As you share with others, be aware that you should talk for no longer than *three* minutes at any one time. Then pause and let the other person share. Slow down and enjoy the conversation. Share with sincerity and with sensitivity, build rapport, and invite friends to share with you at church.

Using Outreach Gifts Appropriately

In the good old days, the preacher would announce that on Monday night we would be visiting out in the community. Folks would gather and go knock on doors of those who had visited the church and needed to join. Some folks would go out "soul-winning" and almost pressuring visitors to accept Jesus as Lord. Both of these approaches to visiting usually made both the visitor and the host somewhat uncomfortable.

What we are discovering today is that most of us don't want to go knock on doors on Monday evenings. Most people aren't welcoming to those visits anyway. We must find ways to contact those who visit our churches with sensitivity, with intentionality, and with consistency. However, we must not suppose that everyone in our neighborhood is opening their doors to "church strangers" dropping in to chat about church. We have found the Internet, e-mail, and the telephone to be effective tools for consistent contacting. We can conduct quick phone visits or e-mails to those who come and visit. In this way, we can visit without being intrusive or insensitive. We can also visit in ways that are comfortable and help us relax as we share.

The type of contact with a visitor varies. In researching outreach efforts through the past 25 years, several types of giftedness have emerged. The percentages shared are unscientific but roughly representative of who does what in your congregation. Understanding these types may help your church find ways to involve your entire congregation in reaching out to visitors and prospects in the community.

Visitation Types—Who Does What?

• *Soul-Winners.* Only about two percent of the people in your church are effective "soul-winners"! These are the people who are comfortable in leading others to faith decisions. While we believe that these decisions are absolutely essential, most of us just don't feel equipped to share an evangelistic message. In fact, most church folks think that the pastor or staff minister should be the ones to do this. If you exhort church members to "win" others to Christ, you are probably frustrated with the low participation in this approach. At the two-percent rate, only two people in a hundred feel equipped, called, comfortable, and willing to share. Yes, we should be sharing our faith. Yes, we should be leading others to saving relationships with Christ. But we have to spend more time training our members and helping them get comfortable before sending them out.

• *Prospectors.* About five percent of your church members are comfortable prospecting in the community. Prospectors are those who will go out into a neighborhood unannounced, knock on doors, and try to identify prospects. While few churches use this approach with frequency and even less with success, again we must train our people if we are going to go "prospecting." Direct mail and target phone calling seem to be much more effective in reaching these neighborhoods today.

• *Enrollers.* About 8 percent of your church members are comfortable asking a prospect to enroll in a Sunday school class or to join the church. Thus, not even all Sunday school teachers feel equipped to do this. While it may seem like a simple invitation, many are uncomfortable with offering this invitation. "Since you've been coming to our class, may we enroll you as a member?" seems an easy question for many. But, again, we must be intentional about training Sunday school leaders how to ask the question at the appropriate time in appropriate situations.

• *Contacters.* Contacting is simply saying "hello" to those who have visited the church. This is perhaps the most comfortable approach of outreach. Yet, only about 25 percent of our church members feel comfortable even making a brief contact. This form of outreach includes note writing and phone calling. Contacting requires little emotional energy. However, only about one fourth of our church members feel comfortable participating in this type of outreach. Train your Sunday school workers to help out in this meaningful form of outreach.

These four types of outreach workers add up to about 40 percent of your church members who feel comfortable participating in an organized outreach ministry. About 50 percent of your church will pray for you as you make outreach visits. That leaves about ten percent of a typical congregation who will not be involved at all in any form of outreach. Actually, that number is probably higher! About 10 percent of the congregation doesn't want any growth or any change at all.

Outreach to prospects means that new people will be joining the church, and for some members, such newness is not welcomed. Not everyone thinks that reaching out to new people is a good idea. Of course, we know better—the gospel is for all people. These people are waiting on the 85–90 percent of our church who will reach out to them. Remember, over 80 percent of those visiting church come because of an invitation from a friend or family member!

Marketplace Evangelism

The term "marketplace evangelism" has been used to describe the relational sharing about Christ that takes place between friends or acquaintances. This "relationship sharing" or "marketplace evangelism" is not new; family and friends have been sharing for years. However, we have become a much more private nation. Our relationships are increasingly guarded and protected. We have to build trust slowly and share with sincerity before we are able to share a convincing witness with someone.

But the world is hungry for a word from God. And "marketplace evangelism" is becoming a normal and acceptable approach to sharing the gospel. The key to the effectiveness of this (and any) evangelistic approach is the level of sincerity with which the message is shared. If we are not sincere in our sharing, the friend with whom we share will know immediately and turn away from us.

One excellent approach to this challenge is called "Hospitality Evangelism." This program, produced by the Church Resources Ministry Group of the Cooperative Baptist Fellowship, is built around establishing relationships with guests and simply sharing hospitality with them when they come to our churches. This is not another program for doing outreach; it is an approach that transforms church members into learning that outreach is a way of life, that visitors to the church are potential friends first and church members second, and that they can become comfortable in sharing their faith. The approach is based on a solid training model that includes a weekend retreat and training event, worship events, and personal devotions. This is an excellent training tool for helping your church members grow more comfortable in sharing with friends and acquaintances.

The main point of awareness is to make outreach a conscious part of our lifestyles and a part of the ongoing church ministry. Outreach is more than a program. Outreach is more than just inviting people you know to church. Outreach is a balanced approach of personal invitation and the use of formal outreach tools. Take every opportunity to build relationships. Take every opportunity to reach out to your community.

Years ago as a youth minister in a small town in Kentucky, every Monday I would sit through three lunch hours at the local high school cafeteria. I didn't hand out tracks; I didn't evangelize; I just sat and listened. The youth from our church would sit with me and introduce their friends to me. This may have been some of the most effective outreach I've ever been a part of. Just sitting and listening communicated a sincere level of care. My consistent presence communicated that they could trust me. We reached a great number of young people for our church's ministries just by "hanging out"!

Outreach ministry comes in many forms. The approaches to how we reach out are not nearly as important as the sincerity and consistency with which we reach out.

Balancing Positive Inreach and Outreach Efforts

Meaningful church growth only happens in the context of intentional vision. This intentional vision means that everyone is made to feel important and vital to the ministries of the church. Everyone, members and nonmembers, Sunday school members and worship participants, first-time visitors and long attending guests, must be made to feel vital to the church. Efforts to include all persons must be ministry-based, people-centered, and sincere. People can spot phony responses quickly. We must present sincere responses to those who participate with us.

People go where they know they have been prepared for and are cared for! As we communicate to all who participate that they are vital, they begin to realize that everything we do in ministry is for others. We prepare for others, we organize for others, we give for the benefit of others. In fact, those churches doing ministry most effectively give equal priorities to members and those who are *not* members.

Outreach helps us focus on those who are not members of our

church. Many churches put all their resources and energy toward bringing in new people. These churches are so busy bringing in new people and baptizing new converts that they forget about teaching and growing those already in the church. These churches focus so much on conversion that they forget about ministry and discipleship. Many churches are so evangelistic that they are seen as open and accepting but not providing much depth for Christian growth.

Inreach helps us focus on members of the church. Many churches put all their resources and energy on keeping people in the church. These churches tend to turn inward and provide many programs and ministries to their members, yet they forget about sharing the gospel with those outside the church. These churches tend to focus so much on "member care" that they forget about the hungry, lost, and hurting around them. Many churches are so devoted to inner ministry that they are seen as deep and highly "spiritual" but not providing much access for those without Christ or a church family.

The key to managing outreach and inreach effectively is balance. When these two elements work in productive tandem with one another, we take care of those who are not members and also take care of those who are. The balanced congregation finds ways to build bridges to those who do not belong and open doors of service for those who do. As we seek balance, we begin to make sure there is a full sense of being, belonging, and becoming.[1]

As we provide a sense of *being*, we let persons know that they can "be" who they are and participate. Our congregations are not country clubs or secret societies. Come and be who you are, find your place, and help us do the ministry of sharing Christ with the world. As we provide a sense of *belonging*, we let persons know that they will find community and family in the church. We all have a deep need to belong to something bigger than ourselves. Many of us are separated by hundreds of miles from our families. We need each other! Come and be who you are and find a family of faith that will nurture you and care for you. As we provide a sense of *becoming*, we let persons know that they will find opportunities for growth and ministry. We all want to make a difference. This drives us to service and sharing. As we serve and share, we grow and we become. Come and be who you are and grow to be the person God created you to be. Come and become who you already are in Christ!

So, how do we communicate "prepared for and cared for," "being, belonging, and becoming"? We make people our primary focus and make sure that everything we do in our churches keeps outreach and inreach in balance. We make sure that in our worship and teaching and service we do all we can to keep outreach and inreach in balance.

Five Approaches to Ensure Balance

(1) The balanced congregation provides multiple entry points for members and prospects to participate. Small groups such as Sunday school classes are excellent ways for people to get connected to your congregation. Worship, music groups, support groups, mission efforts, and work groups all provide opportunities for service and fellowship. These small groups provide an entry way, a connectivity to the life of the congregation.

One excellent approach to being inclusive is the telephone (or e-mail). Every Saturday evening, between the hours of 5pm and 7pm, call every person on your class enrollment. The conversation is simply a 30-second "howdy." "Hello, Jane, this is Bo from the church. I was just finishing up my Sunday school lesson and you were on my mind. (Pause for them to respond whatever they will.) Well, I just wanted to say 'hey' and I'll see you when I see you!" See how simple? No guilt, no manipulation, not even long conversation, this is just a "prepared for and cared for" touch. This is one of the most effective approaches I have ever used. This is still something I use!

(2) The balanced congregation is user-friendly. Presenting an inviting facility with readable and informative signs is crucial to being user-friendly. And the facility is only part of the challenge. We need to clue everyone in to the "inside traditions" and processes that everyone seems to know but no one seems to talk about.

A recent church prospect approached me on a Sunday morning. Their question, "How do I give an offering to your church?" I stood there gaping and gasping! Finally I explained the process of giving both in worship and through the Sunday school. As the prospect walked away, those words kept ringing in my ears. They were ready and willing to share commitment. Our church had been too hung up in a process to provide ease of participation for a prospect!

(3) The balanced congregation is contemporary and relevant. We share the greatest news in the world to the world. But many of us are still sharing the "old, old story" like we live in Jesus' day. We are no longer in the 1950s. We must communicate a congregation that is clued in to the times. The Internet is looming large; we must provide electronic access to our churches. The days of the cell phone and instant messaging are upon us; we must use technology to our benefit. What about "streaming video and audio" of a worship service or Sunday school class?

Secondly, we must be socially, culturally, and spiritually relevant. People come to us asking, "Can you help me cope?" We must find ways to communicate not only in contemporary ways but also with deep meaning. Too many "postmoderns" have turned off the words of the church because they have not found any meaning in our words. Strong leadership, team ministry, value, and quality indicate our relevance in the lives of those who come to us.

(4) The balanced congregation has an attitude for growth. Christian education is the constant process of molding and remolding those who come to us. As people participate in our congregations, we help them enter as they are and grow to who they need to become. And this growth process never ends. We constantly challenge all in our church to grow, to share, and to continue. The balanced congregation embraces change because they understand that this change is the process of upgrade and growth. A church in a "constant upgrade" mode is a church with an aggressive growth mindset. These churches make certain that everyone understands that people *are* the church, not just participants *in* the church!

(5) The balanced congregation has an attitude that everything is education and education is everything! Every ministry, program, and activity that is presented has an element of teaching and an element of worship. Never miss an opportunity to pray and to teach. Never miss an opportunity to speak to the "teachable moment" that arises. Meaningful Christian education happens in the context of intentionality. Don't pass up any opportunity to share and to worship.

So What?

Outreach and inreach are important building blocks for the growing Sunday school. As you touch people with the love of Christ and the ministries of your church, you will bring more and more people to your congregation. As you keep up with people and provide special places for them, your membership not only grows numerically but deeper spiritually. Take care of people. Stay balanced in your ministries. Be sincere and intentional in your sharing. Make a difference in the lives of people in your church and your community.

Trust God, pray daily, and live on bravely!

Note

[1] R. Wade Paschal has further discussion on this in *Vital Adult Learning* (Nashville: Abingdon Press, 1994), 13-22.

Chapter Seven

Building Block 6–Receptivity and Inclusion

The case has been clearly made that the institutional church in America is diminishing in both size and influence. While church leaders and supporters argue against characterizations labeling the present as a "Post-Christian" era and the church as an "archaic institution," the statistics paint a bleak overall picture. Research statistics have come furiously to us in recent days from a variety of reliable sources.

- 66 percent of all Americans are either non-believers or non-church goers.
- 85 percent of today's Protestant churches are either plateaued or in decline.
- 30 percent of adults called themselves spiritual, but not religious.
- 45 percent of adults say they rely on their own personal views, not God and religious teaching, to decide how to conduct life.
- Almost 45 percent believe that if you are a good person, you will go to heaven, whether or not you believe in God.

An important question facing the church is, "Are we receptive to including the unchurched and nonbelievers in our congregation?" The way we respond to the community around us determines how receptive we are. However, one blatant fact confronts us: The church of today has seemingly lost touch with the larger portions of culture and society. And further, the church of today is not very interested in reestablishing itself in the midst of these larger portions.

Is the church no longer open and receptive to persons not of the faith? Does the modern church project an uncaring and non-relevant attitude in a world of rapid change? Where is the distinctiveness that the church once brought to the community? Why are there more people attending community recreation facilities on Sunday morning than the local church? An even more important question facing the church may be "What are we to do about the deteriorating reputation and impact church has on culture and society?" Culture and society, after all, make up the mission field of each and every church.

The answer for the vast majority of churches is first to admit to certain failings, and then go about the business of creating a clean slate of possibilities. This entails taking a deeply personal and critical look at the reasons we do church. It also entails how we treat people once they take a risk and come to church. Ultimately, most churches will face the deepest of all questions—do we do church for ourselves or for people "out there"? Every church that opts for "out there" takes the first steps toward growth, renewal, and true New Testament viability. The model of church we practice is that the church exists as much for those who are *not* members as it does for those who are.

The following steps will be a move away from mainly static tradition to an integration of new possibilities designed for reaching new people. These new possibilities will need to be well thought out, safe, low-stress, relevant, truly user-friendly, easy-to-access, and geared to the unique mission/prospect field of each church.

Quick Disclaimer: There is no one perfect system, format, or plan for a growing Sunday school. You cannot buy a box of Instant Church Growth from the local Christian bookstore. A real temptation exists simply to buy the latest and greatest denominational growth tool and put it into action. Rarely does this approach work. Another temptation is to emulate a successful church by implementing their methodologies, structure, and programming. This approach of "copying" often leads to failure, primarily because what works in one church just might not be the solution for another church. The road to growth is strewn with the remains of many misguided attempts to purchase the latest program or to transfer an innovative approach from one successful church to another that hopes to grow. There are reasons for this disappointing reality.

However, the question still remains, what are we doing to reach the people "out there," and what are we doing to help them assimilate once they come "in here" to the church?

Know Your Mission/Prospect Field

The first order of business for a church that hopes to grow through receptivity and inclusion, especially through the Sunday school, is to learn as much as possible about their unique prospect field. Successful churches regularly spend time and resources in determining who and what makes up the "church field." The "church field" is actually the reasonable geographic areas from which a church can potentially draw people. Then the church programs according to the gathered information. And this is the danger of simply buying "growth in a box" or borrowing a format or style from another successful church.

Successful churches predicate growth on creating programming linked to their unique area of prospects. Chances are, few churches share the exact same prospects, and if they do, other dynamics will be in play that create differences between churches. Picture an old, semirural church that adopts the Willow Creek model (of suburban Chicago) for worship and discipleship. Or a First Baptist Church in a southern county seat town that opts for the Saddleback (California) Community Church approaches. Chances are the outcomes in either situation won't make the same history as Willow Creek or Saddleback have.

The primary key for a church that hopes to grow by attracting new people is to know as much as possible about the people they have the best opportunities of reaching. Following the intelligence gleaned from their research, the church must then program ministries that will meet the unique needs of the possible new members. And the church people must be receptive to opening up their church, their Sunday school classes, and including those who come.

Simply put, a truly successful church always tailors plans for Sunday school and other programming based on the uniqueness of their prospect field. And equally true, a successful church always makes multiple ways for the unchurched to be included. The Greek word for this is *allelon. Allelon* translates "be one another to each other." Scripture is filled with the command to *allelon* one another, to be one another to each other.

People who are not involved in church have yet to experience this fully. When a Christian loves you in the fullness of the love of Christ, something extraordinary happens! Christian love is exemplified in countless casseroles during a hospital recovery, platters of fried chicken during a family tragedy, and tons of cards during both. Christian love is exemplified in the phone calls and personal visits that wish us well when good or bad comes to us. *Allelon* begins to take shape when someone we don't even know goes out of his or her way to initiate care and be concerned with *my* comfort. We have been commanded to "pray for one another"—that's *allelon* in action. We are to "bear up one another's burdens"—yes, that's *allelon* too! Above all of this, we are called to do so with love.

Are we truly receptive to new people coming in to our church? Think carefully before you answer. If new people come to us and growth begins to take shape, these "new folks" will be parking in your space, sitting in your seat, and serving on your committees. If these "new folks" come to us, we'll have higher utility bills, we'll have to buy more Sunday school literature; we may even have to build a bigger building! Do we really want these "new folks" to come?

What are you doing to attract new people to your church? More importantly, what obstacles do you have in place to discourage their attending? What are you doing to encourage new people to join in the fellowship of the church? More importantly, what are you doing to discourage their participation?

Embrace Your Uniqueness

As stated before, there really is no such thing as an "average church." Each church is unique in its location, socio-economic and denominational makeup, levels of spiritual maturity, overall personality, corporate culture, staff and leadership, and facilities. Unfortunately, too many pastors and Christian educators seem dissatisfied with the genuine uniqueness of the churches they serve. This "grass must be greener" mindset has caused several leaders to attempt to make their church something it can't, shouldn't, or doesn't want to be. Sadly, this leader-inflicted flux has also led to a heightened number of unemployed clergy.

In order to grow, a church must first be led to discover, understand, and celebrate its innate uniqueness. Then, and only then, can a church move forward to do the things necessary to attract and facilitate new people.

Six Ways to Embrace Your Uniqueness

(1) Translate Beliefs into Action. Many people in our churches proclaim their faith weekly by their attendance. However, fewer actually move out into active ministry. Find relevant ministries in which church members and prospects can participate. For some, these may be mission projects around your city. This may be participating in a Habitat for Humanity project. This may be helping at a local community center for the homeless or tutoring low-income children after school. There are hundreds of opportunities for translating faith into action across the street from your church, across town, and even around the world. Find some projects and get involved. Invite prospects and the unchurched to join you, and watch what happens.

(2) Build Quality Friendships. People today are looking for genuine and sincere friendships. The Sunday school is the perfect place for this to happen. Provide times for building fellowship both inside the Sunday school hour and outside of class. Plan fellowships that encourage relationship-building. Plan small-group gatherings that allow you time to sit and visit with each other. In the good old days, we spent hours sitting on the front porch, visiting and talking about life. Provide some "front porch" time for quality friendships to develop.

(3) Be Open to Diversity. We live in a time of exciting and diverse cultures. Issues of ethnicity and gender beg to be addressed by the church. Challenge your church to embrace diversity rather than running from it. We can experience a richness of life as we share together. Be open to sharing with each other, to learning from each other, and to experiencing the love of God in the uniqueness of us all.

(4) Express your Spirituality with Openness and Honesty. Too often today, church "folks" try to hide behind their spirituality. They talk with lots of "God talk" and quote Scripture for everything that happens. Prospects and unchurched persons cannot relate to that behavior. Sharing openly and honestly builds trust. We have to find ways to share our faith in the language of everyday reality. Model for your people ways of communicating with one another in everyday speech rather than in the language of the church.

(5) Be User-Friendly. Walk through your building as if you are seeing it for the first time. Do you have signs that direct you easily through the building? How easily can you move to the sanctuary, fellowship hall, and childcare areas? Take a look at the classrooms. How neat and clean is your building? How bright and inviting are your rooms? Walk through the building with your eyes closed. What do you smell? Do the smells of dirty diapers fill your nose in the preschool area? Does old grease jump out at you as you walk through the church kitchen? Clean, bright, inviting spaces welcome prospects and the unchurched into your congregation. Clean-smelling rooms, fresh paint, and uncluttered hallways are easy for people to navigate.

(6) Provide Adequate Space. There is nothing worse than coming into a room of strangers and having to sit on top of one another! The surest way to prevent guests returning to your church is to "pack" them into a room. Church architects suggest that adults need 10–12 square feet to feel comfortable. Youth, children, and preschoolers need at least twice that amount of space. Do a space study of your classrooms. Compare the square footage available with the enrollment of each class using the rooms. If you are using more than 80 percent of the

square footage allowed, participants in the class will feel crowded. If you are using more than 80 percent of your total church space allotment, you are crowded. If space is becoming an issue, either begin thinking about alternative uses of space or building additional space.

Embrace the unique aspects of your church. Find ways to be creative with the space, classrooms, and people in your congregation. As you become comfortable with the special aspects of your fellowship, you will be able to communicate your comfort level to those who come to join in with you.

Blending Innovation and Tradition

Innovative churches are all the rage these days. The reasons for their popularity should not be lost in light of the staggering number of declining churches. Churches open to innovation are more likely to grow and often stand apart from static, traditional churches in fresh, contemporary ways. These churches also seem to be more inclusive, open, inviting, easy-to-access, and actually aware that it is now the twenty-first century. So, what's the secret? Again, there is no secret or one single plan that takes a church from static to successful in reaching new people. The key is simply to use the information gleaned from analyses of the prospect field to create a unique ministry plan designed to attract and facilitate new people.

With all of the rhetoric and attention placed on innovation, a question that begs to be asked is "What place is there for the traditional Sunday school model in a growing church?" The reality is that traditional Sunday school classes work well in most churches. The issue in question is how effective these traditional approaches are in attracting new people, especially non-faith people. Many traditional classes provide community and excellent Bible study for those who already attend, but they aren't very open to inviting and including new people.

Traditional classes provide ministry for "traditional" people and are worthy of inclusion in any attempts to create a climate for Sunday school growth. However, in order to grow through attracting and facilitating new people, a new section of the Sunday school must be tailored to that end. In effect, the Sunday school would have two elements, one traditional element designed primarily for those already involved, and one born out of a need to reach new people.

The options available for innovative approaches to Sunday school are as wide and varied as there are dreamers to dream them into reality. Two examples are shared, not for you to copy, but to spur you to think about how you can be creative in your church.

Johns Creek Baptist Church in the northern metro-Atlanta area provides an example for churches seeking a model for innovative adult Sunday school. In the early 1990s, Johns Creek created a model that stressed Christian community, easy access, user-friendliness, and relevance. With loosely age-graded Communities (classes) designed to provide Christian community and seminars led by facilitators who rotate through the system, Johns Creek has grown beyond all projected expectations. The Johns Creek story proves that a church can pay attention to its prospect field, create programming and ministries tailored to its hoped-for constituency, and have amazing success.

On another plane is Providence Baptist Church in Charlotte, North Carolina. Providence has a traditional Sunday school organization. Classes maintain themselves primarily due to the space available. New classes are started by using "missionaries" from existing classes who are similar in age and stage to the new class demographic. Two to three innovative elective classes are offered each quarter for varying times. Facilitators are enlisted to lead the topical discussions. Participants in the elective classes come out of their existing classes for 8–10 weeks for the elective study. They then return to their ongoing classes at the end of the study. This approach has helped to develop new teachers, to bring back inactive members, and even to form new ongoing units.

As uniquely different as these two Sunday school programs are, they each share basic characteristics that are elemental to long-term success. Each program is designed from the outset with the novice church attender in mind. Paying attention to the entire experience, from the parking lot to the teaching/learning session and beyond, leads to a truly lower stress, easy-to-navigate, user-friendly framework.

While the term user-friendly now seems almost trite, it remains a prime determinate of overall success for most organizations.

Keeping the novice or non-faith attender in mind will also allow for a concentration on relevance. It is important to provide Bible studies that can be contextualized into the world of today. That is, after all, where we exist. The relevance dilemma may be the most difficult facing today's church. A Barna Group study found that only one-fourth of Americans strongly agree that "the Christian churches in my area are relevant to the way I live today."[1]

Leonard Sweet puts an edgier spin on the need for relevance in reaching today's non-believer:

> Theology is not boring . . . Dorothy Sayers states, "It is the dogma that is the drama, not beautiful phrases, nor comforting sentiments, nor vague aspirations to loving kindness." Postmodern Christianity must engage the intellect, must have edge, must be conversant with the sciences, and must not be afraid of intellectual fire.[2]

Once the innovative Sunday school has paid proper attention to the novice attender's overall experience and created a truly relevant atmosphere for spiritual growth, one essential element remains: Care for one another. Ministry and member care for each class participant are of supreme importance. This means that any innovative format must include provisions to take care of ministry needs in small groupings. This element can, and must, be foundational in all programs.

So What?

Despite the depressing fact that the majority of Protestant churches are stagnant or in negative growth cycles, there is hope for almost any church to reverse this process. This hope rests with altered visions of the church's reason for existence and a recommitment to taking the age-old message to a new world in ways that it can and will understand. If there was ever a need for old wine in new wineskins it is today. Tomorrow may be one day too late.

How willing are you to re-invent your approach to your church's ministry? There are parts of your tradition that need to be done away with. There are innovations to your ministry that need to be added. Cleaning out is never easy. Adding on is never easy, either. But neither is serving God easy! The Bible is filled with stories of people who had tremendous opportunities to make a difference and squandered those opportunities. Our prayer is that your church will thrive in the midst of blending tradition with innovation. Our prayer is that you will build with the building blocks that have been suggested. Our prayer is that you will grow and reach out and still be relevant 100 years from now!

Grow for it! What have you got to lose? And think of all that there is to be gained. The world is waiting desperately for us to reach out. You won't succeed in all that you attempt. However, you won't fail in all that you attempt either. Put this book down and do something significant for the Kingdom of God. Don't get discouraged when things don't work out exactly as you planned. Those planned outcomes rarely happen. Keep trying. Keep praying. Keep growing. And remember, when you're falling on your face, you're actually moving forward.

Trust God, pray daily, and live on bravely!

Notes

[1] George Barna, *The Barna Report: What Americans Believe* (Ventura CA: Regal Books, 1991), 49.

[2] Leonard Sweet, *SoulTsunami* (Nashville: Zondervan, 1999), 57.

Chapter Eight

Keep On Keeping On!

No, the Bible teaching ministry through the Sunday school is not dead. The organization is not in shambles. The leadership capabilities of teachers and other leaders are still vital for growing churches. The same factors that made "Flake's Formula" such a success in the last 100 years are still at work. The only ingredient missing is just a bit of innovation.

The Sunday school has been, is still, and will continue to be one of the strengths of church ministry. But we must continue to do what we know to do:

- to inspire with a great vision
- to keep balance in the ministry
- to lead with intentionality, developing others, growing yourself
- to teach God's Word with relevance and creativity
- to reach out to the community and to reach in to one another
- to be receptive and inclusive to those who join us

These building blocks are in no way offered as a prescription for growth. The six building blocks outlined in this work will help you grow *if* you plan and then work the plan. We urge you to take what is pertinent and apply that to your setting. Make these building blocks personal for your church and congregation. Don't take these as another "Church Growth Quick" plan! They were not intended for that.

These building blocks are shared as tools for evaluating your church setting and guiding your church toward more intentional planning. As you evaluate your church setting, keep building on those elements that you consider your strengths. As you evaluate your church setting, train in those areas that you consider not as strong. Keep on working toward what you know to do. Keep on working on areas that you know need to improve.

- Be more caring.
- Communicate that everyone is vital.
- Be more contemporary and relevant.
- Honor tradition without being bound by it.
- Embrace innovation without losing distinctiveness.
- Continually evaluate ministries and strive for quality.
- Continually train existing leaders and develop new ones.
- Be intentional about doing the work of the Sunday school.
- Dream great things.
- Attempt great things.
- Make 100 things 1 percent better.

Remember, people go where they know they've been prepared for and are cared for. We may not restore the Sunday school to the greatness of the past, but it won't be for lack of effort! As we work toward the goal of growth, we will grow. We may not grow at the levels of some of the examples shared, but we will grow.

You Already Have the Tools

The building blocks are just another set of tools for helping your Sunday school and church to grow. You have had the tools in your hands already. The question is not, "Will these tools work?" The more relevant question is perhaps, "Are you willing to work with these tools?" The way you answer this question determines what happens in your congregation. If you are willing to work, your church will grow. If you are only willing to maintain the status quo, your church may even experience some growth—at least enough to keep the membership from moving into decline. However, if you are not willing to do anything more than what you are doing now, you can almost count on decline.

We are all now living in a very different world from that of the 1950s. Most of us are living in a very different world since the 1980s! The way we cope with and handle change determines how well we emerge into this next decade. Are we really a people of faith? Or are we more a people of formula? The answers are yet to be determined.

God is not the God who plays it safe. Since the beginning of time, God has taken risks. God has built the Kingdom on people like Moses, David, Simon Peter, Saul turned Paul, and you and me! God has modeled risk-taking; God has modeled honoring tradition. You and I can do no less. Take the best of what your church has been offering over the past 50 years and polish that up. Treat these traditions with respect and with sensitivity. But don't be bound by the past, by the "way we've always done it before"!

Take the best of what our world now offers and "baptize" this for the church. Use these innovations for your church and for growing your congregations. There are risks in being innovative, but don't be afraid of a little risk. Be careful how you introduce change; be sensitive to the changes you make. But don't be paralyzed into doing nothing because of a little risk. The days ahead are exciting. These building blocks can be helpful tools in preparing for "what's next." Or this can just be another Sunday school book that gathers dust on your shelf. The choice of how you use this writing is up to you.

The one best approach listed in almost every management book, church growth book, and innovation book is *work hard*. Working hard means working long hours. Working hard means sacrificing other parts of our lives for the mission and the goal. Working hard means that we will be intentional about getting the work done. One of our concerns in writing this has been that too many of us don't want to work hard anymore. Remember, these tools are not bound together into a magic wand! You have to *work hard* to grow your church and to grow your Sunday school. Our prayer is that you will take our tools, work hard, and reach more people than ever before for the cause of Christ.

Very few churches are going to thrive into the next century. We are too nice to sweat, too proud to cry, too sophisticated to laugh, too busy to celebrate! Growing churches will let down their guards and begin to share in meaningful and intimate ways. Growing churches will plan for intentional interaction and fellowship times. Growing churches will comfort those who cry and celebrate with those who succeed. And growing church must laugh. Lord, let us laugh!

And as we grow, trust God, pray daily, and live on bravely!